crochet FOR mindfulness

crochet FOR mindfulness

creative projects to help you be in the moment, relieve stress, and manage pain

emma leith

CICO BOOKS

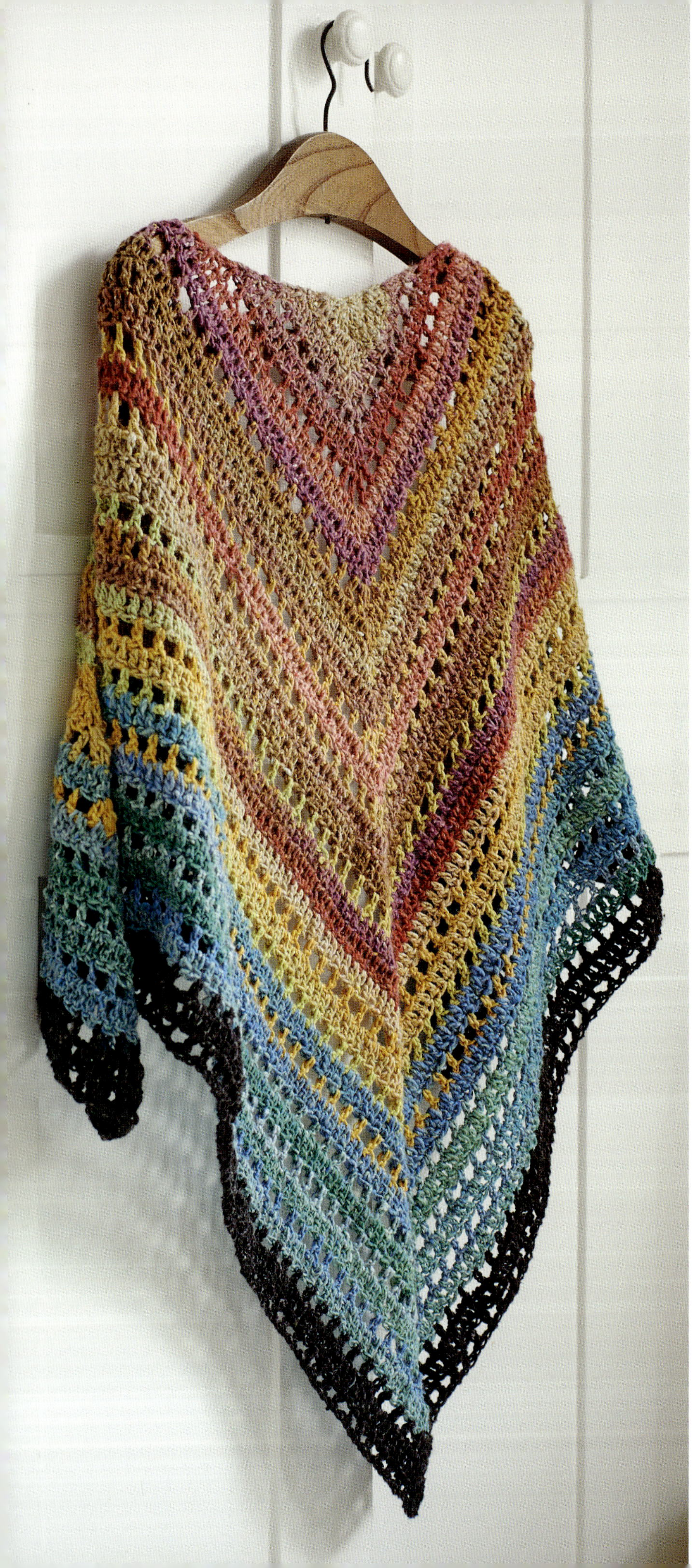

To Lili.
My fiercest critic and guiding light.

This edition published in 2026
by CICO Books
An imprint of Ryland Peters & Small Ltd
1452 Davis Bugg Road,
Warrenton, NC 27589
www.rylandpeters.com

First published in 2019 as *Mindful Crochet*

10 9 8 7 6 5 4 3 2 1

US Library of Congress CIP data has been applied for.

ISBN: 978-1-80065-574-4

Printed in China

Editor: Marie Clayton
Pattern checker: Jemima Bicknell
Designer: Alison Fenton
Photographer: James Gardiner
Stylist: Nel Haynes
Illustrator: Stephen Dew

Senior designer: Emily Breen
Art director: Sally Powell
Creative director: Leslie Harrington
Production manager: Gordana Simakovic
Publishing manager: Carmel Edmonds

contents

introduction

Crochet has changed my life and I hope it will yours, too. It is the doorway to my happy place where pain and anxiety are softened and a state of peaceful acceptance resides. Crochet kept me grounded when the cancer diagnosis spun my world off its axis and it continues to help me with my pain on a daily basis. It doesn't make the bad stuff go away, but it can help transform it.

If you take one thing away from this book, let it be this. Nothing is ever wasted. There is value in everything. The time spent making something that doesn't work out—a pattern gone wrong, a color combination that doesn't hit the mark—none of this matters because it's all part of the journey and we learn something with every stitch. Our body holds on to the memory of the movement, so enjoy it all for what it is in that moment and let the hook guide you on your way. All you need to succeed with crochet is the playful desire in your heart to hook. Keep going no matter what and let the magic happen.

Happy hooking!

a note on yarns

Multicolored yarns are sometimes discontinued, and even within existing ranges there can be a lot of variety within shades, so your projects may not look exactly like the photos but they will still be beautiful and colorful.

a note on skill levels

Each project includes a star rating as a skill level guide and listed below is an overview of the techniques needed:

• Easy projects requiring only basic crochet skills.

•• Slightly more challenging projects with repetitive stitch patterns, simple shaping, or using join-as-you-go.

••• Advanced projects using a variety of techniques and more complex stitches.

chapter 1

color therapy

mandala curtain

Think of each mandala as a mini-make—it can be completed in under 30 minutes and be picked up and put down anytime. If your narrative is that you're no good with color, now's the time to change that—these colors work together in any combination, so experiment and play a little. Maybe try a color grouping you wouldn't normally do and see how it unfolds.

SKILL RATING: ● ● ●

MATERIALS:

Rico Ricorumi DK (100% cotton, approx. 63yds/58m per ⅞oz/25g ball) light worsted (DK) weight yarn

1 ball each of:
- Yellow shade 006
- Candy Pink shade 012
- Fuchsia shade 014
- Lilac shade 017
- Purple shade 020
- Tangerine shade 026
- Orange shade 027
- Emerald shade 042
- Light Green shade 046
- Grass Green shade 044
- Sky Blue shade 031
- Blue shade 032

US size E/4 (3.5mm) and US size G/6 (4mm) crochet hooks

Yarn needle

Sewing needle and thread

FINISHED MEASUREMENTS:

Mandala: 2½in (6.5cm) diameter

Curtain: 38½in (98cm) long, 28in (71cm) wide

GAUGE (TENSION):

Exact gauge is not important on this project.

ABBREVIATIONS:

See page 127.

FOR THE CURTAIN

MANDALA (make 36—6 per strand)

Use any sequence of colors.
Using first color and US size E/4 (3.5mm) hook, make a magic ring, or ch6 and join with ss in first ch to form a ring.
Round 1: Ch3 (counts as first dc), 11dc into the ring, join with ss in 3rd of beg 3-ch. *12 sts.*
Fasten off.
Round 2: Join second color in any st, ch2 (counts as 1sc and ch1), [1sc in next st, ch1] 11 times, join with ss to beg 1-ch. *12 sc + twelve 1-ch sps.*
Fasten off.
Round 3: Join third color in any 1-ch sp, ch2 (counts as first hdc), 1hdc in same sp, [2hdc in next 1-ch sp] to end, join with ss in 2nd of beg 2-ch. *24 sts.*
Fasten off.
Round 4: Join fourth color in any st, ch1 (does not count as sc), [2sc in next st, 1sc in next st] 12 times. *36 sts.*
Fasten off.

BEADS (make 36—6 per strand—in assorted colors)

Leaving 8in (20cm) end at beg to use as stuffing for bead, using US size E/4 (3.5mm) hook, make a magic ring, or ch6 and join with ss in first ch to form a ring.
Round 1: Ch1, 6sc into the ring. Do not join, work in a continuous spiral.
Round 2: 2sc in each st around. *12 sts.*
Round 3: 1sc in each st around.
Round 4: [1sc, skip next st] 6 times. *6 sts.*
Stuff bead with beg yarn end.
Round 5: [1sc, skip next st] 3 times, join with ss in first sc.
Fasten off, thread yarn end through bead and back through again to secure.

MAKING UP AND FINISHING

For strand A, choose two strands of yarn to hold together and work as one "chunky" strand. Thread 6 beads onto the chunky strand—do not thread the yarn through the middle of the bead but rather through one stitch only.
With both strands held together and using US size G/6 (4mm) hook, ch17, bring first bead up to the hook and ch the next stitch around it to secure, *ch25, bring the next ball up to the hook ch around the bead as before; rep until all 6 beads are secured, ch17.
Fasten off.
Make 2 more strand A.

For strand B, choose two strands of yarn to hold together and work as one "chunky" strand. Thread 6 beads onto the chunky strand as before.
With both strands held together and using US size G/6 (4mm) hook, ch35, bring first bead up to the hook and ch the next stitch around it to secure, *ch25, bring the next ball up to the hook ch around the bead as before; rep until all 6 beads are threaded.
Fasten off.
Make 2 more strand B.

Starting from the top on the 35-ch section of strand B, use the needle and thread to sew a mandala approximately 3in (7.5cm) before the first bead. Repeat on each strand B. Sew the remaining mandalas midway on each 25-ch section between beads on all strands A and B.

Choose two strands of yarn to hold and work as one "chunky" strand.
With both strands held together and using US size G/6 (4mm) hook, ch10, join with a ss in 10th ch from hook to form hanging loop, ch10, *join top end of strand A with 1sc, ch15, join top end of strand B with 1sc, ch15; rep until all 6 strands are joined, ch20, join with a ss in 10th ch from hook to form hanging loop.
Fasten off.

Sew in all yarn ends carefully.

- **Use the US size G/6 (4mm) crochet hook when working with 2 strands together.**

colorplay table runner

The pleasure of this piece lies in how the colors go together; each works in harmony with any other, so no matter what combination you use the finished piece will be a work of beauty. I've also played with different textures and finishes—the Catona has a shiny finish that is set off beautifully alongside the soft stone washed cotton. Each yarn brings out the unique quality of the other, making this piece a real treasure.

SKILL RATING: ● ● ●

MATERIALS:

Scheepjes Catona (100% cotton, approx. 67yds/62m per ⅞oz/25g ball) fingering (4 ply) weight yarn
 1 ball each of:
  Crystalline shade 385
  Powder Pink shade 238
  Apple Granny shade 513
  Tangerine shade 281
  Delphinium shade 113
  Lilac Mist shade 399
  Yellow Gold shade 208

Scheepjes Stone Washed (78% cotton, 22% acrylic, approx. 142yds/130m per 1¾oz/50g ball) sport (5 ply) weight yarn
 1 ball each of:
  Tourmaline shade 836
  Forsterite shade 826
  Amazonite shade 813
  Beryl shade 833
  Lilac Quartz shade 818
  Rose Quartz shade 820
  Pink Quartzite shade 821

US size G/6 (4mm) crochet hook

Yarn needle

FINISHED MEASUREMENTS:

38in (96.5cm) long, 12in (30.5cm) wide

GAUGE (TENSION):

One square = 2¼in (6cm) square, using US size G/6 (4mm) hook.

ABBREVIATIONS:

See page 127.

FOR THE RUNNER

FOUNDATION SQUARE ROW 1

Using any color of Catona, make a magic ring, or ch6 and join with ss in first ch to form a ring.
Round 1: Ch3 (counts as first dc), 11dc into the ring, join with ss in 3rd of beg 3-ch. *12 sts.*
Fasten off.
Round 2: Join any color of Stone Washed in any st, ch2 (counts as first hdc throughout), 1hdc in same st, *2hdc in each of next 2 sts, (2hdc, ch2, 2hdc) in next st (corner); rep from * twice, 1hdc into each of next 2 sts, (2hdc, ch2) into beg st, join with ss in 3rd of beg 3-ch.
Fasten off.

SECOND SQUARE ROW 1

Using any color of Catona, make a magic ring, or ch6 and join with ss in first ch to form a ring.
Round 1: Ch3 (counts as first dc), 11dc into the ring, join with ss in 3rd of beg 3-ch. *12 sts.*
Fasten off.
Round 2: Join any color of Stone Washed in any st, ch2, 1hdc in same st, *2hdc in each of next 2 sts, (2hdc, ch2, 2hdc) in next st (corner); rep from * twice, 1hdc into each of next 2 sts, (2hdc, ch1) into beg st, remove hook from loop, with RS facing throughout insert hook in any corner of foundation square, pick up loop again, pull through 2-ch corner of foundation square (joins two squares), ch1, join with ss in 3rd of beg 3-ch of second square.
Fasten off.
Make 3 more squares, joining each to prev square as set for row of 5 joined squares.

SIXTH SQUARE ROW 2

Rep second square, joining to second corner of foundation square in round 2.

ALL SUBSEQUENT SQUARES

Rep second square to end of round 1.
Round 2: Join any color of Stone Washed in any st, ch2, 1hdc in same st, 2hdc in each of next 2 sts, (2hdc, ch2, 2hdc) in next st (2nd corner), 1hdc in each of next 2 sts, (2hdc, ch1) in next st, remove hook from loop, with RS facing throughout insert hook in corner of prev square in same row, pick up loop again, pull through 2-ch corner of square to join, (ch1, 2hdc) in same st to complete 3rd corner, 1hdc in each of next 2 sts, (2hdc, ch1) in next st, remove hook from loop, with RS facing throughout insert hook in corner of matching square in prev row, pick up loop again and pull through 2-ch corner of square to join, ch1, join with ss in 3rd of beg 3-ch of original square.
This links 3 squares on 2 corners.
Cont as set until you have 16 rows of 5 squares.
Fasten off.

MINDFULNESS

Notice if there is a certain color combination that you gravitate toward and whether this changes depending upon how you are feeling—do your spirits lift or thought patterns change as your color combinations emerge from the hook?

BORDER

Use any 2 colors of Stone Washed—I have opted for Pink Quartzite for round 1 and Tourmaline for round 2.
Round 1: Join first color in corner sp of any side square, ch2 (counts as first hdc), 1hdc in same sp, skip next hdc, 1hdc in each of next 5 sts, skip joined corner and first hdc of next square, 1hdc in each of next 5 sts, (2hdc, ch2, 2hdc) in next corner, cont around as set, working (2hdc, ch2, 2hdc) in each of the two outer corner spaces of each corner square, ending with (2hdc, ch2) in beg sp, join with ss in 2nd of beg 2-ch.
Fasten off.
Round 2: Join second color in corner sp of any side square, ch1 (counts as 1sc), 1sc in same sp, *skip next hdc, 1sc in each of next 5 sts, skip 3 sts, 1sc in each of next 5 sts, (2sc, ch2, 2sc) in corner sp; rep from * around, working an additional (2sc, ch2, 2sc) in the second outer corner of each corner square, ending with (2sc, ch2) in beg sp, join with ss in beg 1-ch.
Fasten off.

MAKING UP AND FINISHING

Sew in all yarn ends carefully.

This piece will need to be blocked to ensure it lays flat and looks its best.

shisha mirrored valance

Having a blast of happiness that frames your doorway or window can sometimes be just the tonic on those gloomy days. I love working with these little mirrors and enjoy seeing the light reflect and bounce around the room, adding sparkle to the crochet. This piece is designed to be worked in stages, making small elements that are joined together at the end, so this is a "pick up and put down" project.

MINDFULNESS

These colors all work together in any combination so be inspired by what you see and follow your heart. You may decide to go heavy on the blues and greens, which will result in a cooler feel to the finished piece but will be just as cheery. Let the colors work their magic as you crochet your squares, and notice the effects they have on your thoughts and mood.

SKILL RATING: ● ● ●

MATERIALS:

For the valance:

Scheepjes Catona (100% cotton, approx. 68yds/62.5m per ⅞oz/25g ball) fingering (4 ply) weight yarn

1 ball each of:

- Shocking Pink shade 114
- Fresia shade 519
- Lavender shade 520
- Tangerine shade 281
- Yellow Gold shade 208
- Lime Juice shade 392
- Jade shade 514
- Cyan shade 397
- Electric Blue shade 201

Scheepjes Catona (100% cotton, approx. 136yds/125m per 1¾oz/50g ball) fingering (4 ply) weight yarn

1 ball of Bridal White shade 105

US size F/5 (3.75mm) crochet hook

Yarn needle

81 small glass beads

For the mirror frames:

Scheepjes Maxi Sweet Treat (100% cotton, approx. 153yds/140m per ⅞oz/25g ball) lace weight yarn

1 ball each of:

- Cyan shade 397
- Electric Blue shade 201
- Vivid Blue shade 146
- Jade shade 514

US size B/1 (2mm) crochet hook

34 shisha mirrors

FINISHED MEASUREMENTS:

32in (81cm) long, 9in (23cm) deep

GAUGE (TENSION):

19 sts x 24 rows = 4in (10cm) over single crochet, using US size F/5 (3.75mm) hook and Scheepjes Catona.

ABBREVIATIONS:

See page 127.

SPECIAL ABBREVIATION:

bead picot: ch1, bring bead to hook, ch1 around bead, ch1, ss in first ch

FOR THE VALANCE

SQUARES (MAKE 8)

Using first color and US size F/5 (3.75mm) hook, make a magic ring, or ch6 and join with ss in first ch to form a ring.

Round 1: Ch2 (counts as first hdc throughout), 11hdc into the ring, join with ss in 2nd of beg 2-ch. *12 sts.*

Round 2: Ch2, 1hdc in same st, 2hdc in each st to end, join with ss in 2nd of beg 2-ch. *24 sts.*
Fasten off first color.

Round 3: Join second color in any st, ch2, (1hdc, ch2, 2hdc) in same st as join (corner), *1hdc in each of next 5 sts, (2hdc, ch2, 2hdc) in next st (corner); rep from * twice, 1hdc in each of next 5 sts, join with ss in 2nd of beg 2-ch. *36 sts + four 2-ch sps.*
Fasten off second color.

Round 4: Join third color in any corner 2-ch sp, ch1 (counts as first sc throughout), (1sc, ch2, 2sc) in same sp as join, *skip next st, 1sc in each of next 8 sts, (2sc, ch2, 2sc) in next corner 2-ch sp; rep from * twice, skip next st, 1sc in each of next 8 sts, join with ss in beg 1-ch. *48 sts + four 2-ch sps.*
Fasten off third color.

Round 5: Join fourth color in any corner 2-ch sp, ch1, (1sc, ch2, 2sc) in same sp as join, *skip next st, 1sc in each of next 11 sts, (2sc, ch2, 2sc) in next corner 2-ch sp; rep from twice, skip next st, 1sc in each of next 11 sts, join with ss in beg 1-ch. *60 sts + four 2-ch sps.*
Fasten off fourth color.

- The shisha mirrors are available online.
- To fix the valance to either a door or window frame, sew the loop half of a strip of hook and loop tape to the WS of the top band. Then attach the hook half of the tape to the surface from which you wish to hang your crochet.

Round 6: Join fifth color in any corner 2-ch sp, ch2, (1hdc, ch2, 2hdc) in same sp as join, *skip next st, 1hdc in each of next 14 sts, (2hdc, ch2, 2hdc) in next corner 2-ch sp; rep from * twice, skip next st, 1hdc in each of next 14 sts, join with ss in 2nd of beg 2-ch. *72 sts + four 2-ch sps.* Fasten off.

TRIANGLE FLAG (MAKE 8)

Take any square and with RS facing and using US size F/5 (3.75mm) hook, join yarn into any 2-ch sp corner.

Row 1: Ch1 (counts as first sc), 1sc in each of next 18 sts. *19 sts.*

Row 2: Turn, ch1 (does not count as st), skip first st, 1sc in each st to last 2 sts, sc2tog. *17 sts.*

Rows 3–10: Rep row 2. *1 st.*

Fasten off.

MAKING UP AND FINISHING

Lay the squares down in a line in any sequence you like, with their triangle flags at the bottom. Using the yarn needle and matching yarn, and with squares RS tog, join the squares into a strip using whip stitch (see page 125). Do not join the triangle flags.

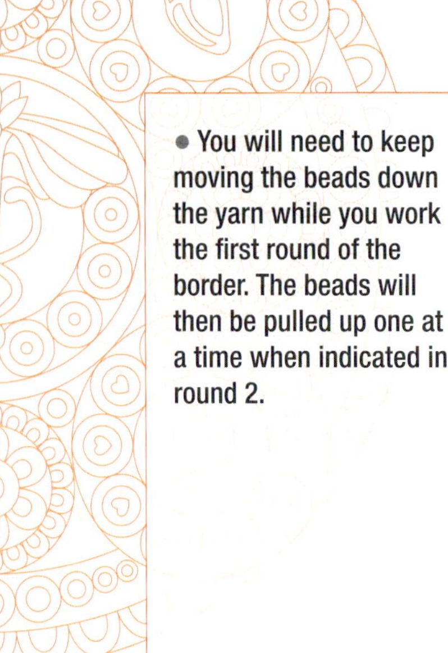

• You will need to keep moving the beads down the yarn while you work the first round of the border. The beads will then be pulled up one at a time when indicated in round 2.

WHITE BEADED BORDER

Thread 81 glass beads onto Bridal White, push down until needed. With RS facing and using US size F/5 (3.75mm) hook, join yarn at top right corner sp of crochet strip.

Round 1: Ch1 (counts as 1sc throughout), 1sc in each st along top edge to corner working 1sc into each square join (152 sts), (1sc, ch1, 1sc) in corner sp, skip next st of square, 1sc in each of next 17 sts along side edge of square, *1sc in each row end to tip of triangle (9 sts), (1sc, ch1, 1sc) in tip of triangle, 1sc in each row end to top of triangle (9 sts); rep from * on all triangles, 1sc in each of next 17 sts along side edge of square, ch1, join with ss in beg 1-ch.
Round 2 (beaded round): Ch1, 1sc in each st along top edge to corner sp, (1sc, ch1, 1sc) in corner sp, 1sc in each of next 17 sts, *[bead picot, 1sc in each of next 2 sts] 4 times, bead picot, 1sc in next st, (1sc, bead picot, 1sc) in tip of triangle, [1sc in each of next 2 sts, bead picot] 4 times, 1sc in each of next 3 sts (3rd sc is in st joining two triangles); rep from * along all triangles, bead picot, 1sc in each of next 17 sts along side edge of square, (1sc, ch1) in beg corner, join with ss into beg 1-ch.
Do not fasten off.

TOP BAND

Row 1: Ch1 (counts as first sc), ch1, skip next st, *1sc, ch1, skip next st; rep from * to last st, 1sc in last st, changing to next color on last sc.
Row 2: Ch2, [1sc in next 1-ch sp, ch1, skip next st] to end, 1sc in last 1-ch sp, changing to next color on last sc.
Rows 3–9: Rep rows 1 and 2, changing color on each row.
Rows 10–12: Using one color only, ch1, 1sc in each st and sp to end.
Fasten off.

SINGLE MIRROR FRAMES (MAKE 26)

Using any Maxi Sweet Treat yarn and US size B/1 (2mm) hook, make a magic ring.
Round 1: Ch1 (does not count as st throughout), 24sc into the ring, ss in first sc. *24 sts.*
Fasten off first color. Pull yarn end to tighten ring but leave enough space to view mirror through.
Round 2: Join second color, ch1, [2sc in next st, 1sc in each of next 5 sts] 4 times, ss in first sc to join. *28 sts.*
Fasten off.

Position the frame in place on the main panel of squares and oversew (see page 124) halfway around using the round 2 color. Slide the mirror under the frame and finish sewing the frame to the panel.

DOUBLE MIRROR FRAMES (MAKE 8)

To make the double-sided mirror frames to hang underneath each triangle, make 16 single frames as above (2 for each mirror). Place with WS together, matching stitches around the edge, and join with a single crochet seam (see page 124), working 2sc in every seventh stitch and using yarn to match round 2. Insert two mirrors back to back into frame when about halfway around, then complete the seam and join with a ss in the first sc.
Fasten off, leaving a 20cm (8in) end. Sew the double-sided mirror into the stitch at the peak of each triangle in round 2 of the beaded border.

Sew in all yarn ends carefully.

squares and circles stool cover

This cover is designed to fit a square stool. I like to sit and make all the colorful circles first. If you are new to the join-as-you-go method, then I recommend you sit quietly with no distractions whilst you practice this simple technique of joining two squares as you crochet the side. Essentially you are slip stitching two squares together between each three-double crochet cluster, instead of making the chain.

MINDFULNESS

Once you're familiar with the pattern for the first three rounds the repetition becomes a meditation in itself and you can begin to observe your thoughts and feelings as you work. Letting go of all judgment, simply observe and be in your body. This is the beauty of colorful circles!

SKILL RATING: ● ● ●

MATERIALS:

Rico Creative Cotton Aran (100% cotton, approx. 92yds/85m per 1¾oz/50g ball) worsted (Aran) weight yarn

1 ball each of:

- Natural shade 60 (MC)
- Candy Pink shade 64
- Tangerine shade 76
- Banana shade 68
- Violet shade 16
- Sky Blue shade 37
- Light Green shade 40
- Light Pistachio shade 44

US size 7 (4.5mm) crochet hook

Yarn needle

FINISHED MEASUREMENTS:

To fit a 13in (33cm) square stool

GAUGE (TENSION):

Rounds 1–2 of 3-color circle = 2½in (6.5cm) diameter, using US size 7 (4.5mm) hook.

ABBREVIATIONS:

See page 127.

FOR THE COVER

3-COLOR CIRCLES (make 9)

Using first color, make a magic ring, or ch6 and join with ss in first ch to form a ring.

Round 1: Ch3 (counts as first dc throughout), 11dc into the ring, join with ss in 3rd of beg 3-ch. *12 sts.*

Fasten off first color.

Round 2: Join second color in any st, ch3, 1dc in same st, [2dc in each st] to end, join with ss in 3rd of beg 3-ch. *24 sts.*

Fasten off second color.

Round 3: Join third color in any st, ch3, 1dc in same st, 1dc in next st, [2dc in next st, 1dc in next st] 11 times, join with ss in 3rd of beg 3-ch. *36 sts.*

Fasten off third color.

Lay out circles in 3 rows of 3 in desired order.

When turning circles into squares you will join each square from left to right.

FIRST LARGE SQUARE

Round 4: Join MC in any st of any circle, ch3 (counts as first dc), 2dc in same st, ch1, *skip 2 sts, 3hdc in next st, ch1, skip 2 sts, 3hdc in next st, ch1, skip 2 sts, (3dc, ch2, 3dc) in next st (corner); rep from * twice, skip 2 sts, 3hdc in next st, ch1, skip 2 sts, 3hdc in next st, ch1, skip 2 sts, (3dc, ch2) in beg st (fourth corner), join with ss in 3rd of beg 3-ch.

Fasten off.

JOINING LARGE SQUARES

Round 4: Join MC in any st of next circle, ch3 (counts as first dc), 2dc in same st, ch1, skip 2 sts, 3hdc in next st, ch1, skip 2 sts, 3hdc in next st, ch1, skip 2 sts, 3dc in next st, join with ss in corresponding corner of starting square by inserting hook in corner sp of starting square from underneath, 1sc in corner sp of starting square (counts as first of 2-ch for corner sp), ch1, work 3dc in same st of current square as prev 3-dc to complete corner. Cont to join squares tog with 1sc in next side sp of starting square, 3dc in next side sp of current square. Cont replacing each 1-ch at sides of current square with 1sc in next side sp of starting square to next corner and then replace first of 2-ch at corner sp of current square with 1sc in corner sp of starting square to finish joining the side. Complete the current square as normal, following round 4 of first large square above.

When joining a square to 2 prev squares, replace both corner ch of current square with 1sc in each adjoining square. Cont working join-as-you-go method (see page 122) to make one large panel of 3 by 3 squares.

SMALL SIDE SQUARES (make 24)

Using any color, make a magic ring, or ch6 and join with ss in first ch to form a ring.

Round 1: Ch3 (counts as first dc throughout), 11dc into the ring, join with ss in 3rd of beg 3-ch. *12 sts.*

Fasten off first color.

Round 2: Join MC in any st, ch3, 2dc in same st, skip 2 sts, (3dc, ch2, 3dc) in next st (corner), skip 2 sts, 3dc in next st, using join-as you-go method as above, starting in any corner of main panel, join with 1sc onto corner sp of first large square on main panel, ch1, 3dc in same st as prev 3-dc, join with 1sc onto next side sp of main panel square, skip 2 sts, 3dc in next st, join with 1sc onto next sp of main panel square, ch1, 3dc in same st as prev 3-dc, skip next 2 sts, (3dc, ch2) in beg st (fourth corner), join with ss in 3rd of beg 3-ch.

Cont to join squares on round 2 in this way, make and join 2 small side squares to each large square (6 small squares per side). After working the first square on each side, join each subsequent square in this way to one side of the prev small square, as well as the main panel square.

Fasten off.

MINI CIRCLES FOR BORDER (make 24)

Using any color, make a magic ring, or ch6 and join with ss in first ch to form a ring.

Round 1: Ch1 (counts as first sc throughout), 7sc into the ring, join with ss in beg 1-ch. *8 sts.*

Fasten off first color.

Round 2: Join second color in any st, ch1, 1sc in same st, 2sc in each st to end, join with ss in beg 1-ch. *16 sts.*

Fasten off, leaving 4in (10cm) end.

MAKING UP AND FINISHING

Oversew (see page 124) the sides of the two adjoining small squares together at each corner to bring the sides down to form the stool top shape.

BOTTOM EDGING

Round 1: Join MC in right-hand corner sp of any small square, ch1 (counts as first sc), *skip next st, 1sc in each of next 5 sts, 1sc in corner sp of square, 1sc in corner sp of next square; rep from * to last square, skip next st, 1sc in each of next 5 sts, 1sc in corner sp of last square, join with ss in beg 1-ch.

Round 2: Ch1, [1sc in each of next 5 sts, sc2tog] 24 times.

Fasten off.

Thread the yarn end of a mini circle onto the yarn needle and sew to hang at the base of the cover at one corner. Repeat at each corner, then add five more evenly spaced along each side.

Fasten off and sew in all yarn ends carefully.

MINDFULNESS

This pattern is designed to let you explore your relationship with color and to try out new color combinations. The beauty of crochet is that it's only crochet, so if you decide you don't like something you can rip it out and start again. It's trying new ideas out that's important—if we don't try we will never know! So often in life we limit ourselves by our own thoughts and judgments, so allow yourself the time and space to work with color without an attachment to outcome.

texture place mats

These mats are made with one of my all time favorite stitches, and when worked with two strands of yarn held together the density and woven texture is amplified—making this the perfect stitch for place mats. The beauty of this pattern is that once the foundation row is established you will be working in the chain spaces throughout, making it a smooth and restful crochet experience.

SKILL RATING: ● ● ●

MATERIALS:

Rico Creative Cotton Aran (100% cotton, approx. 92yds/85m per 1¾oz/50g ball) worsted (Aran) weight yarn

1 ball each of:

- Natural shade 60
- Rose shade 00
- Candy Pink shade 64
- Fuchsia shade 13
- Light Blue shade 32
- Sky Blue shade 37
- Light Green shade 40
- Light Pistachio shade 44
- Banana shade 68
- Tangerine shade 76
- Orange shade 74

US size J/10 (6mm) crochet hook

Yarn needle

FINISHED MEASUREMENTS:

9½in (24cm) wide, 8¼in (21cm) long

GAUGE (TENSION):

15 sts x 14 rows = 4in (10cm) over patt, using US size J/10 (6mm) hook and two strands of yarn held together.

ABBREVIATIONS:

See page 127.

FOR THE PLACE MATS

Hold two strands of different colors tog throughout.

Using any two colors held tog, ch38.

Row 1: 1sc in 4th ch from hook, *ch1, skip next st, 1sc in foll st; rep from * to end, changing to next 2 colors on last sc, turn. *18 sc + eighteen 1-ch sps.*

Row 2: Ch2 (counts as 1 ch sp), 1sc in first 1-ch sp, *ch1, 1sc in next 1-ch sp; rep from * to end, changing to next 2 colors on last sc, turn.

Rep row 1 until 31 rows have been worked. Fasten off, leaving 6in (15cm) ends.

MAKING UP AND FINISHING

To secure the yarn ends, gather the four strands per row together and tie in a double knot. Lay the mat flat and trim the ends to make a 1in (2.5cm) long fringe on each side.

- Adjust the size to suit your plates—but always start with an even number of chain.
- Change color on each row on the last yarn round hook of the current row. Leave 6in (15cm) yarn ends when joining and fastening off to make the fringe later.
- To create a subtle pattern that pleases the eye without being noticeably obvious, work every third row with a cream and a pastel shade held together.

boho bunting

Lift the spirits with this gloriously happy bunting, featuring colors that ping and pop against the contrast of bold black and white. The magic of this project is in the color, so note how each color makes you feel. Does the use of black and white alter your response to a particular color? As you focus your mind toward the interplay of colors can you begin to see preferences and patterns emerging?

MINDFULNESS

Each triangle can be completed in a half-hour sitting and there's no rush. This project requires a little bit of counting on each round, so practice making the counting slow and rhythmical. Slowing the stitches slows the mind and the breath.

SKILL RATING: ● ● ●

MATERIALS:

Scheepjes Cahlista (100% cotton, approx. 92yds/85m per 1¾oz/50g ball) worsted (Aran) weight yarn

1 ball each of:

- Jet Black shade 110 (A)
- Bridal White shade 105 (B)
- Shocking Pink shade 114
- Tulip shade 222
- Lemon shade 280
- Yellow Gold shade 208
- Tangerine shade 281
- Apple Granny shade 513
- Cyan shade 397
- Delphinium shade 113

US size 7 (4.5mm) crochet hook

Yarn needle

FINISHED MEASUREMENTS:

Bunting: 69in (175cm) long, 6½in (16.5cm) deep

GAUGE (TENSION):

Rounds 1–3 = 2¾in (7cm) diameter, using US size 7 (4.5mm) hook.

ABBREVIATIONS:

See page 127.

SPECIAL ABBREVIATION:

esc (elongated single crochet): insert hook in st two rows below current row, yo, pull yarn up level to current row, yo, pull through both loops on hook to complete esc

FOR THE BUNTING

TRIANGLES (make 7)

Using the first color, make a magic ring, or ch6 and join with ss in first ch to form a ring.

Round 1: Ch3 (counts as first dc throughout), 11dc into the ring, join with ss in 3rd of beg 3-ch. *12 sts.*

Fasten off first color.

Round 2: Join A in any st, ch2 (counts as first hdc), 1hdc in same st, [2hdc in next st] 11 times, join with ss in 2nd of beg 2-ch. *24 sts.*

Fasten off A.

Round 3: Join B in any st from row 1, pull yarn up to current row and ch1 (counts as first esc), [1sc in next st, 1esc in next st] 11 times, join with ss in first esc. *12 sc + 12 esc.*

Fasten off.

Round 4: Join second color in any st, ch1 (counts as first sc), [ch2, skip next st, 1sc in foll st] 11 times, ch2, skip last st, join with ss in beg 1-ch. *12 sc + twelve 2-ch sps.*

Fasten off second color.

Round 5: Join third color in any 2-ch sp, ch3, 2dc in same sp, [3hdc in next 2-ch sp] 3 times, (3dc, ch2, 3dc) in next sp (first corner), [3hdc in next 2-ch sp] 3 times, (3dc, ch2, 3dc) in next sp (second corner), [3hdc in next 2-ch sp] 3 times, 3dc into beg 2-ch sp, ch2, join with ss in 3rd of beg 3-ch (third corner).

Fasten off.

Round 6: Join B in any corner 2-ch sp, ch1 (counts as first sc), [ch3, skip next 2 sts, 1sc in foll st] 4 times, ch3, (1sc, ch2, 1sc) in next corner 2-ch sp, [ch3, skip next 2 sts, 1sc in foll st] 4 times, ch3, (1sc, ch2, 1sc) in next corner 2-ch sp, [ch3, skip next 2 sts, 1sc in foll st] 4 times, ch3, 1sc in beg 2-ch sp, ch2, join with ss in beg 1-ch.

Fasten off B.

Round 7: Join fourth color in any corner 2-ch sp, ch1 (counts as first sc), *[(1sc, 2hdc, 1sc) in next 2-ch sp] 5 times, (1sc, 1hdc, ch1, 1hdc, 1sc) in next corner 2-ch sp; rep from * once more, [(1sc, 2hdc, 1sc) in next 2-ch sp] 5 times, (1sc, 1hdc, ch1, 1hdc) in beg corner 2-ch sp, join with ss in beg 1-ch.

Fasten off fourth color.

MAKING UP AND FINISHING

Sew in all yarn ends carefully.

JOIN THE TRIANGLES

Row 1: Using B, ch15, join with ss to beg ch to form hanging loop, ch10, *with triangle RS facing, 1dc in any 2-ch sp corner, [ch3, skip next 3 sts, 1sc in foll st] 5 times, ch3, 1dc in next 2-ch sp corner, ch5; rep from * until all 7 triangles are joined, ch25, join with ss in 15th ch from hook to form hanging loop.

Row 2: Ch1 (does not count as st throughout), 1sc in each st and ch to start of beg hanging loop.

Fasten off B.

Row 3: Join A in first sc, ch1, 1sc in each st to end.

Fasten off A.

Row 4: Join B in first sc, ch1, *1sc, 1esc in next st from row 1; rep from * to end.

Fasten off and sew in yarn ends.

- Mix and match the colors to suit your mood whilst following this simple color pattern: row 2 is always black, rows 3 and 6 are always white. Everything else is up to you—but just remember to change color with every round!

- Cotton holds its shape well, making it perfect for bunting, but as always with worsted (Aran) cotton take it slow because the yarn can split and there's not a lot of springy softness to it.

MINDFULNESS

Learning to be playful and to test things out is so important in both crochet and life! By loosening up on needing everything to be perfect every time, you'll develop a softer mindset and learn to relax into it. Sometimes wonderful things happen when you just go with the flow—if you don't try you will never know!

prayer flag garland

This is the ultimate stash buster project where anything goes! Once completed these prayer flags are small enough to be hung just about anywhere and will bring a little happiness wherever they are. Making colorful crochet pieces to decorate and adorn your living space can have a positive impact on your mental health. These crochet creations are imbued with the pleasure associated with crochet and give meaning and value as well as sparkles of color to your home.

SKILL RATING: ● ● ●

MATERIALS:

Rico Ricorumi DK (100% cotton, approx. 62yds/57m per ⅞oz/25g ball) light worsted (DK) weight yarn

Small amount each of:

- Cream shade 002 (A)
- Orange shade 027 (B)
- Fuchsia shade 014 (C)
- Sky Blue shade 031
- Grass Green shade 044
- Blue shade 032
- Light Green shade 046
- Tangerine shade 026
- Yellow shade 006
- Lilac shade 017

Rico Essentials Cotton DK (100% cotton, approx. 142yds/130m per 1¾oz/50g ball) light worsted (DK) weight yarn

Small amount each of:

- Violet shade 97
- Aqua shade 95
- Pistachio shade 86

Rico Fashion Cotton Metallise (53% cotton, 35% acrylic, 12% metallic, approx. 142yds/130m per 1¾oz/50g ball) light worsted (DK) weight yarn

Small amount of:

- Silver shade 004

US size G/6 (4mm) crochet hook

Yarn needle

FINISHED MEASUREMENTS:

39½in (100cm) long

GAUGE (TENSION):

Each flag = 2¾in (7cm) wide, 3½in (9cm) long, using US size G/6 (4mm) hook.

ABBREVIATIONS:

See page 127.

SPECIAL ABBREVIATION:

esc (elongated single crochet): insert hook in st two rows below current row, yo, pull yarn up level to current row, yo, pull through both loops on hook to complete esc

FOR THE GARLAND

FLAGS (make 7)

When changing color, introduce new color on last yo of final st of current row and leave 6in (15cm) ends. Work over both yarn ends when working next row, except as indicated.

Using any color, ch14.

Row 1: 1hdc in 3rd ch from hook, 1hdc in each ch to end, changing to next color on last st, turn. *12 sts.*

Row 2: Ch2 (does not count as st throughout), 1hdc in each st to end, changing to next color on last st, turn.

Do not work over both yarn ends when working row 3.

Row 3: Ch3 (does not count as a st), skip st at base of ch, 1hdc in next st, [ch1, skip next st, 1hdc in foll st] 5 times, changing to next color on last st, turn.

Row 4: Ch2, 2hdc in each 1-ch sp from prev row ending with 2hdc in last sp between beg 3-ch and hdc from prev row, changing to next color on last st, turn.

Row 5: Ch1 (does not count as st throughout), 1sc in each st to end, changing to next color on last st, turn. *12 sts.*

Row 6: Ch1, [1sc, 1esc] to end, changing to next color on last st, turn. *6 sc + 6 esc.*

Do not work over both yarn ends when working row 7.

Row 7: Rep row 3.

Row 8: Rep row 4.

Row 9: Rep row 5.

Row 10: Rep row 2.

Row 11: Rep row 5.

Fasten off.

MAKING UP AND FINISHING

Sew in all yarn ends from rows 2 and 7. For the ends that have been worked over there should be little ends poking out the other end of the row. Gently pull to tighten up the flag and cut off the excess end.

JOIN THE FLAGS

Using A, ch15, join with ss in beg ch to make first hanging loop, ch10, *with RS facing, 1sc in each st along top edge of flag (12 sts), ch10; rep from * until all 7 flags are joined, ending last rep with ch25, join with ss in 15th ch to make second hanging loop,

Next row: Ch1, 1sc in each st and ch to to beg of first hanging loop.

Fasten off.

Cut a length of B and C, each 12in (30cm) longer than the length of the garland just made. With both strands in a yarn needle, thread through one end of the garland and secure with a knot. Weave in and out of each sc of the garland to the other end.

Fasten off.

Sew in all yarn ends carefully.

ADD THE TASSELS

Cut lengths of each color approx. 2½in (6.5cm) long. Holding one strand of two colors together, make a tassel (see page 125). Attach one tassel to the first and last stitches of the bottom edge of a flag, and space another four tassels equally between them. Repeat for the other flags. Trim the tassels to the desired length.

- **Work any light worsted (DK) yarn you have, in any color combination—I changed color for each row. Keeping these flags small means you can use up all those little scraps of yarn, making it no big deal to experiment with color and just pull out a row if you don't like the result.**
- **The pattern can be adapted to make larger flags by simply increasing the foundation chain in multiples of two.**

neon sunburst color-pop bag

The colors in this project are designed to wake up your senses and elevate your playful spirit! This is a great stashbuster project—you can use up all those scraps of yarn left over from other makes.

MINDFULNESS

As you work notice the colors surrounding your stitches and how they are working alongside each other. This will help you consider the next color to use, while also giving you permission to play and experiment. It's all about leaving your comfort zone and trying something new, about approaching things (color in this instance) differently and seeing what emerges from your hook (and life!).

SKILL RATING: ● ● ●

MATERIALS:

Stylecraft Special DK (100% acrylic, approx. 322yds/295m per 3½oz/100g ball) light worsted (DK) weight yarn
 1 ball each of:
  Black shade 1002 (A)
  Cream shade 1005 (B)
  Bright Green shade 1259
  Sherbet shade 1034
  Aspen shade 1422
  Cloud Blue shade 1019
  Turquoise shade 1068
  Bluebell shade 1082
  Lobelia shade 1825
  Wisteria shade 1432
  Violet shade 1277
  Lipstick shade 1246
  Fiesta shade 1257
  Jaffa shade 1256
  Sunshine shade 1114
  Spring Green shade 1316
  Candyfloss shade 1130
  Saffron shade 1081
  Fondant shade 1241

Rico Fashion Cotton Metallise (53% cotton, 35% acrylic, 12% metallic, approx. 142yds/130m per 1¾oz/50g ball) light worsted (DK) weight yarn
 1 ball each of:
  Gold shade 003
  Silver shade 004

US size G/6 (4mm) crochet hook

Yarn needle

Jute bag or similar

Sewing needle and thread

1⅜in (3.5cm) pompom maker

1 large wooden bead per tassel

1 key ring hook per tassel

FINISHED MEASUREMENTS:

12 x 12 x 7¼in (30 x 30 x 18cm)

GAUGE (TENSION):

Five 3-dc groups x 9 rows = 4in (10cm) square over patt, using US size G/6 (4mm) hook.

ABBREVIATIONS:

See page 127.

FOR THE BAG

SQUARE CENTER (make 2)

Using any color, ch6 and join with ss in first ch to form a ring.
Round 1: Ch3 (counts as first dc throughout), 2dc into ring, *ch3, 3dc in ring; rep from * twice more, join with ss in 3rd of beg 3-ch.
Fasten off first color.
Round 2: Join second color in any corner 3-ch sp, ch3, 2dc in same 3-ch sp (half corner made), *ch1, (3dc, ch2, 3dc) in next 3-ch sp (corner made); rep from * twice more (changing to third color halfway through 3rd corner), ch1, 3dc in same sp as beg half corner, ch2, join with ss in 3rd of beg 3-ch.
Fasten off.
Round 3: Join fourth color in any corner 2-ch sp, ch3, 2dc in same 2-ch sp (half corner made), *ch1, 3dc in next 1-ch sp, ch1, (3dc, ch2, 3dc) in next 2-ch sp (corner made); rep from * twice more (changing to fifth color halfway through 3rd corner), ch1, 3dc in next 1-ch sp, ch1, 3dc in same sp as beg half corner, ch2, join with ss in 3rd of beg 3-ch.
Fasten off.

FRONT AND BACK SQUARES (make 2)

Rounds 4–12: Cont to work patt as in round 3, changing color as desired, working 3dc in each 1-ch sp, separated by 1-ch, and (3dc, ch2, 3dc) in each corner 2-ch sp.
Round 13: Join A in any corner 2-ch sp, ch1 (counts as first sc throughout), [1sc in each st and 1-ch sp to next corner 2-ch sp, (1sc, ch2, 1sc) in corner 2-ch sp] 3 times, 1sc in each st and 1-ch sp to beg corner 2-ch sp, 1sc in corner 2-ch sp, ch2, join with ss in beg 1-ch and change to B.
Round 14: Using B, ch1, [1sc in each st to next corner 2-ch sp, (1sc, ch2, 1sc) in corner 2-ch sp] 3 times, 1sc in each st to beg corner 2-ch sp, 1sc in corner 2-ch sp, ch2, join with ss in beg 1-ch and change to A.
Fasten off B.
Round 15: Using A, rep row 14.
Fasten off.

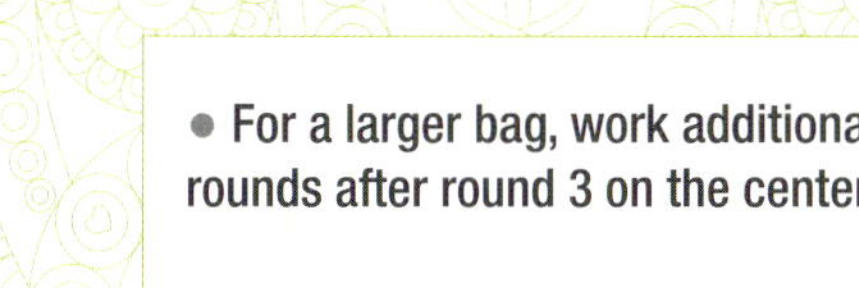

- For a larger bag, work additional rounds after round 3 on the center.

SIDE PANELS (make 3)

You'll work and join squares for sides and base using join-as-you-go method (see page 122).

Make 1 square (starter square A) by working rounds 1–5 as above.
Make 1 square (side square B) by working rounds 1–4 as above.

Join side square B to the starter square A working join-as-you-go method as foll:
Round 5: Ch3, 2dc in same 2-ch sp (half corner made), ch1, (3dc, ch1) in each 1-ch sp to next corner 2-ch sp, 3dc in corner 2-ch sp. Then, instead of making ch2 for corner sp, insert hook in corner sp of starter square from underneath, 1sc in corner 2-ch sp of starter square (counts as first of 2-ch for corner sp), ch1, 3dc in corner 2-ch sp of second square to complete the corner.

To cont joining squares, instead of ch1 work 1sc in next side sp of starter square, 3dc in next side sp of second square. Cont replacing each ch1 at side of second square with 1sc in next side sp of starting square, and replacing first of ch2 at corner sp of current square with 1sc in corner sp of starter square. When second square has been joined to starting square along one side, cont around to finish final round of current square as normal.
Fasten off.

Round 6: Cont to work patt as in round 3, working around entire edge of side panel and treating the "corner" spaces on each side of join as 1-ch sps.
Fasten off.
Round 7: Using A, rep round 13 of front and back squares.
Round 8: Using B, rep round 14 of front and back squares.
Round 9: Using A, rep round 15 of front and back squares.
This makes one side panel. Make 3 more side panels.

MAKING UP AND FINISHING

Sew in all yarn ends carefully.

JOIN SIDES TO FRONT AND BACK

Align one large square and one side panel with WS together. Join any color yarn in corner 2-ch sp of both squares and work a single crochet seam (see page 124).
Fasten off.
Rep to add the other 2 side panels, then join the ends of the side panels.

Add the other large square on the other edge of the side panels to complete the bag.

Place the jute bag inside the crochet bag and sew whip stitch (see page 125) around the top edge to secure in place.

POMPOM TASSEL

Make 4 pompoms (see page 125), leaving 12in (30cm) ends. Using any combination of yarn colors, wrap yarn thickly around a 4in (10cm) piece of cardstock. Cut a 10in (25cm) length of yarn, slide it under the strands and tie in a knot at the top. Remove the tassel from the card, and bind it securely just below the top, using a contrasting color of yarn.

Thread beads onto the end at the top of a tassel, add the first pompom, thread on more beads, then add the second pompom. Secure the yarn end to a key ring hook. Repeat for the second tassel, then clip both to one side of the bag.

MINDFULNESS

Make this a meditative practice by slowing everything down and making each movement purposeful and deliberate. We live in a world that is always on the move, so let this be about the journey and not the destination. Just for now the end point is not important; simply work each component part in isolation as and when you find the time, and then savor the delight of bringing them all together to create happiness in a hoop!

happy flowers chandelier

This colorful hanging decoration will really brighten up any room. Let this project take you on a little journey toward a happier way of being. One small circle can be made in minutes so there's no need to rush.

SKILL RATING: ● ● ●

MATERIALS:

For the chandelier:
Scheepjes Cahlista (100% cotton, approx. 92yds/85m per 1¾oz/50g ball) worsted (Aran) weight yarn
1 ball each of:
Bridal White shade 105 (A)
Jet Black shade 110 (B)
Apple Granny shade 513
Lemon shade 280
Cyan shade 397
Crystalline shade 385
Bluebird shade 247
Shocking Pink shade 114
Tangerine shade 281
Royal Orange shade 189
Lavender shade 520

Scheepjes Catona (100% cotton, approx. 27yds/25m per ⅜oz/10g ball) fingering (4 ply) weight yarn
1 ball each of:
Lemon shade 280
Icy Pink shade 246
Sweet Orange shade 411
Shocking Pink shade 114
Cyan shade 397
Apple Granny shade 513
Lavender shade 520
Lilac Mist shade 399

Anchor Artiste Metallic (80% viscose, 20% polyester, approx. 109yds/100m per ⅞oz/25g ball) fingering (4 ply) weight yarn
1 x ball of Gold shade 300

For the pompoms:
Stylecraft Special DK (100% acrylic, approx. 322yds/295m per 3½oz/100g ball) light worsted (DK) weight yarn
1 x ball of Cream shade 1005

US size G/6 (4mm) crochet hook

Stitch marker

Yarn needle

Polyester toy filling

10in (25cm) inner embroidery hoop (part without metal fastening)

1⅜in (3.5cm) and 2¼in (5.5cm) pompom makers

FINISHED MEASUREMENTS:

Approx. 32in (81cm) total hanging depth, 10in (25cm) diameter

GAUGE (TENSION):

One mini disc = 1¼in (3cm) diameter, using US size G/6 (4mm) hook.

ABBREVIATIONS:

See page 127.

FOR THE CHANDELIER

MINI DISCS (make 95 in total—40 for top, 45 for bottom)

Using any color of Cahlista, make a magic ring, or ch6 and join with ss in first ch to form a ring.

Round 1: Ch3 (counts as first dc), 11dc into ring, join with ss in 3rd of beg 3-ch. *12 sts.*

Fasten off and sew in ends.

BALLS (make 15 in total: 10 for top, 5 for bottom)

Using any color of Cahlista, make a magic ring, or ch4 and join with ss in first ch to form a ring.

Round 1: Ch1 (does not count as st), 6sc into the ring. *6 sts.*

Work in a continuous spiral. PM in last st and move up as each round is finished.

Round 2: 2sc in each st to end. *12 sts.*

Rounds 3 and 4: 1sc in each st to end.

Keep RS facing as the edge begins to curve up.

Round 5: [1sc in next st, sc2tog] 4 times. *8 sts.*

Insert toy filling.

Round 6: [Sc2tog] 4 times. *4 sts.*

Fasten off leaving a 10cm (4in) end, draw end through all rem sts and pull tight.

FLOWERS (make 10)

Using B, make a magic ring, or ch6 and join with ss in first ch to form a ring.

Round 1: Ch3 (counts as first dc), 9dc into the ring, join with ss in 3rd of beg 3-ch. *10 sts.*

Round 2: Using any color of Cahlista and Artiste Metallic held together as one strand, join yarn in any st, ch4 (counts as first sc and ch3), skip next st, [1sc in next st, ch3, skip next st] 4 times, join with ss in first of beg 4-ch. *5sc + five 3-ch sps.*

Fasten off.

Round 3: Using any color of Cahlista and Catona held together as one strand, join yarn in any 3-ch sp, *ch4, (3tr, ch4, ss) in next 3-ch sp (petal made); rep from * 4 more times. *5 petals.*

Fasten off.

MAKING UP AND FINISHING

Sew in all yarn ends carefully.

SUSPENDING STRINGS (make 5)

Cut a 96in (240cm) length each of A and B, hold them together and thread onto a yarn needle.
Work with both yarns as one strand and leaving 8in (20cm) at the end without the yarn needle, ch6. Fasten off to create a knot. Fasten off to create a knot after every section of ch as you continue.
Thread the yarns through the center of 1 ball, then bring the ball down to sit on top of the length of chain. Ch6, thread the yarns through the center of 1 disc, bring the disc down to sit on top of the length of ch. Ch2, thread on a second disc, ch2, thread on a third disc.
Ch6, thread on a second ball, ch6, thread on a fourth disc, [ch2, thread on a disc] 4 times.
Fasten off, leaving a 16in (40cm) end.

POMPOMS

Using A, make five 1⅜in (3.5cm) pompoms and one 2¼in (5.5cm) pompom.

ASSEMBLING THE TOP

Using the 8in (20cm) yarn end, tie each suspending string to the wooden hoop ensuring they are evenly spaced around. Hold all the strings together at the top and adjust so the ring is evenly balanced when it hangs. Tie the ends together in one large knot.

At the top there are now 10 strands (5 in A, 5 in B). Cut off 8 strands above the large knot, leaving 1 in A and 1 in B. Thread the 2¼in (5.5cm) pompom onto these and bring the pompom down to just above the large knot. Using the 2 remaining strands, ch20, ss in first ch to make a loop to suspend the chandelier.

BOTTOM STRINGS (make 10)

Cut a 28in (70cm) length each of A and B, hold them together and thread onto a yarn needle.
Work with both yarns as one strand, tie a knot 10in (25cm) along from the end without the yarn needle.
Thread the yarns through the center of 1 disc, then bring the disc to sit next to the knot. *Leave approx. ⅜–¾in (1–2cm) gap then tie another knot and thread on the next disc; rep from * once more to add a third disc, finishing with a final knot.
Do not trim strands—leave the remaining thread.

ASSEMBLING THE BOTTOM

Using the 10in (25cm) yarn end, tie each bottom string to the wooden hoop, centered between pairs of the top strings.

Working on adjacent pairs of strings, take one strand from the left and one from the right and bring them together to meet directly beneath the suspending string. Tie together and thread all 4 strings one by one through a 1⅜in (3.5cm) pompom. Tie a knot beneath the pompom and cut one strand of A and one of B. Thread the remaining 2 yarns through the yarn needle and thread through the center of 1 disc, then bring the disc to sit approx. ⅜–¾in (1–2cm) below the pompom. Secure with a knot as before, then add 2 more discs spaced and knotted in the same way, ending with a knot. Thread on a ball at the end and secure with a final knot. Thread the remaining ends back up through the ball and trim off. Repeat for remaining 4 bottom strings.

Sew the flowers to the frame, ensuring each flower is placed directly over the points where the top and bottom strings are tied to the hoop.

chapter 2

touch and texture

MINDFULNESS

Enjoy the sensory pleasure as the soft featherlight mohair yarn passes through your fingers. It acts as a gentle balm and can be just the thing to distract you from nagging pain or an anxious mind.

drifting thoughts corsage

Play and have fun with these flowers—there is no right or wrong, so relax and go with the flow, watching the yarn colors emerge with every stitch. Align your breath with your stitches and slow it all down. Allow thoughts to bubble up and float in and out with each petal; don't hold onto them, just let them pass without judgment. Explore this pattern using different yarns and hook sizes and see what emerges. Sew a brooch pin onto the back of your finished flower and you have the perfect gift.

SKILL RATING: ● ● ●

MATERIALS:

Hedgehog Fibres Sock Yarn (90% merino wool, 10% nylon, approx. 437yds/400m per 3½oz/100g hank) fingering (4 ply) weight yarn

Small amount each of:
- Banana Legs
- Birthday Cake
- Villain
- Juniper
- Pinky Swear

Rico Essentials Super Kid Mohair Loves Silk (70% mohair, 30% silk, approx. 218yds/200m per ⅞oz/25g ball) sport (5 ply) weight yarn

¼ ball each of:
- Vanilla shade 047
- Fuchsia shade 021
- White shade 001
- Aqua shade 006

US size G/6 (4mm) crochet hook

Yarn needle

FINISHED MEASUREMENTS:

Approx. 3in (7.5cm) diameter

GAUGE (TENSION):

Exact tension is not important on this project.

ABBREVIATIONS:

See page 127.

SPECIAL ABBREVIATION:

4-tr cl (4-treble cluster): *[yo] twice, insert hook in st, yo, pull a loop through, yo, pull through 2 loops on hook, yo, pull through 2 loops on hook; rep from * 3 more times in same st (5 loops on hook), yo, pull though all 5 loops to complete cluster

FOR THE FLOWER

Hold one strand of sock yarn and one of mohair yarn tog throughout.

Using any 2 colors, make a magic ring, or ch6 and join with ss in first ch to form a ring.

Round 1: Ch3 (counts as first dc), 11dc into the ring. *12 sts.*

Fasten off.

Round 2: Join 2 contrast colors in FLO of any st, *ch3, 4-tr cl in FLO of next st, ch3, ss in FLO of next st; rep from * 5 more times. *6 petals.*

Note how the petals curl in on themselves.

Round 3: Ss in BLO (behind first petal), ch3 (counts as first dc), 1dc BLO in same st, 2dc BLO in each st to end, join with ss in 3rd of beg 3-ch. *24 sts.*

Round 4: *Ch3, 4-tr cl in next st, ch3, ss in each of next 2 sts; rep from * 7 more times. *8 petals.*

Fasten off.

MAKING UP AND FINISHING

Sew in all yarn ends carefully.

● Move slowly through your stitches and keep your tension just so. Unraveling kid mohair is tricky so be sure to get it right first time; it's a good idea to practice the pattern with some spare light worsted (DK) yarn first.

MINDFULNESS

Let this pattern ground you on days when anxiety is high; allow yourself time to focus on the pleasure of making the stitches pop, whilst occupying the working memory with the simple pattern.

mad hatter's tea cozy

Combine a crazy pop of color with a texture stitch and you have a tea cozy to brighten the gloomiest of days. Once you master the stitch you can relax into the pattern and enjoy the pleasure of seeing this cozy come to life. The delight of working the stitch can lift the spirits no end—there is something about running your fingers across the little bumps that feels both satisfying and pleasant in equal measure. This pattern is suitable for those who have mastered double crochet and are confident in the classic granny square.

SKILL RATING: ● ● ●

MATERIALS:

Stylecraft Special DK (100% acrylic, approx. 322yds/295m per 3½oz/100g ball) light worsted (DK) weight yarn
- 1 ball each of:
  - Sunshine shade 1114 (A)
  - Spring Green shade 1316 (B)
  - Cream shade 1005 (C)
  - Black shade 1002 (D)
  - Lavender shade 1188 (E)
  - Fiesta shade 1257 (F)

US size G/6 (4mm) crochet hook

Yarn needle

FINISHED MEASUREMENTS:

8¾in (22cm) wide, 8¾in (22cm) tall

GAUGE (TENSION):

Rounds 1 and 2 = 2in (5cm) diameter, using US size G/6 (4mm) hook.

ABBREVIATIONS:

See page 127

SPECIAL ABBREVIATION:

PC (4-dc popcorn): work 4dc all in same st, remove hook from loop and insert in top of first dc, pick up dropped loop again, yo and join with a ss, pull tight so popcorn pops forward

FOR THE TEA Cozy

SIDE 1

Using A, make a magic ring, or ch6 and join with ss in first ch to form a ring.

Round 1: Ch3 (counts as first dc throughout), 11dc into the ring. *12 sts.*

Fasten off.

Round 2: Join C in any st, ch3 (counts as first dc of PC throughout), complete PC in same st, *ch2, PC in next st; rep from * to end, join with ss in 3rd of beg 3-ch. *12 PC + twelve 2-ch sps.*

Fasten off.

Round 3: Join D in any 2-ch sp, ch3, complete PC in same sp, ch3, PC in same sp (first corner), *[ch2, PC in next st] twice, ch2, (PC, ch3, PC) in next 2-ch sp (next corner); rep from * twice, [ch2, PC in next st] twice, ch2, join with ss in first 2-ch sp of round. *16 PC + twelve 2-ch sps + four 3-ch sps.*

Fasten off.

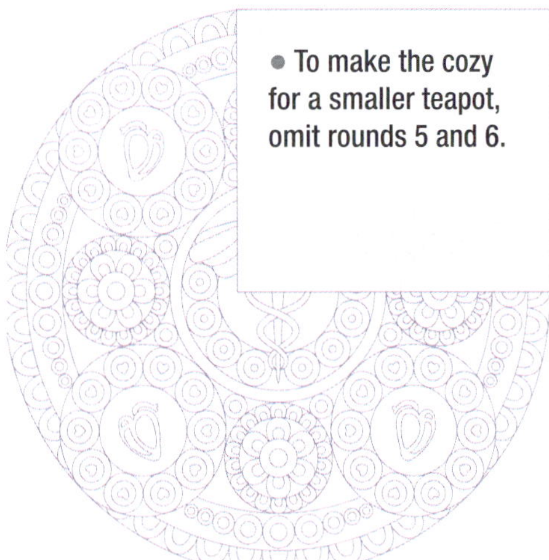

• To make the cozy for a smaller teapot, omit rounds 5 and 6.

Round 4: Join E in any 3-ch corner sp, ch3, complete PC in same sp, ch3, PC in same sp (first corner), *(ch2, PC) in each 2-ch sp to next corner, ch2, (PC, ch3, PC) in next 2-ch sp (next corner); rep from * twice, (ch2, PC) in each 2-ch sp to end, ch2, join with ss in first 2-ch sp of round. *20 PC + sixteen 2-ch sps + four 3-ch sps.*
Fasten off.
Notice how the work is curving slightly to fit around the contours of your teapot.
Round 5: Using F, rep round 4. *24 PC + twenty 2-ch sps + four 3-ch sps.*
Round 6: Using B, rep round 4. *28 PC + twenty-four 2-ch sps + four 3-ch sps.*
Round 7: Using C and D, rep round 4 alt colors to work one PC in C and next in D, carrying yarn not in use and changing color on first ch after each PC. *32 PC + thirty-two 2-ch sps + four 3-ch sps.*
Round 8: Join A in any sp, ch3, 3dc in same st, complete PC in same sp, (ch2, PC) in each 2-ch or 3-ch sp around (no corners on this round), ending with ch2, join with ss in first 2-ch sp of round. Fasten off. *32 PC + thirty-two 2-ch sps.*
Round 9: Join F in any sp, ch1 (does not count as st), 2sc in each 2-ch sp around, join with ss in first st. *64 sts.*
With RS facing, using F, work surface crochet (see page 126) around outer edge of round 1.
Fasten off.

SIDE 2

Using B, make a magic ring, or ch6 and join with ss in first ch to form a ring.
Round 1: Using B, rep round 1 of side 1.
Round 2: Using D, rep round 2 of side 1.
Round 3: Using C, rep round 3 of side 1.
Round 4: Using A, rep round 4 of side 1.
Round 5: Rep round 5 of side 1.
Round 6: Using E, rep round 4 of side 1.
Round 7: Rep round 7 of side 1.
Round 8: Using B, rep round 8 of side 1.
Round 9: Rep round 9 of side 1.
With RS facing, using F, work surface crochet around outer edge of round 1.
Fasten off.

MAKING UP AND FINISHING

Place both sides around the teapot with RS facing outward. Line up the "corners" and, using F, sew them from the base to the bottom of the spout (approx. three popcorns). Leaving a space large enough to fit comfortably over the spout, sew all the way round to the top of the handle. Fasten off.

Sew in all yarn ends carefully.

Make a pompom (see page 125) in F and sew onto the top.

peaceful pillow cover

This project is close to my heart as it's the exact same yarns and pattern I worked whilst recovering from breast cancer. The hook and yarn are easy to hold and the pattern (once mastered) flows gently and requires nothing more than a little peace and quiet as you count the stitches in each round. One circle was all I could manage in a sitting, but seeing the colors fall from the hook gave me the boost I needed whilst having treatment. I've chosen pure merino wool for the border colors to compliment the pure wool Noro, because sometimes a little luxury is what we need to feed the spirit and soul.

MINDFULNESS

Switch off from all decision making and let this glorious yarn do all the talking. Sit back and relax as you create circles of color following this simple rhythmical pattern. After making the circles, discover the delight of seeing how the colors are transformed by either the black or white yarn.

SKILL RATING: ● ● ●

MATERIALS:

Noro Kureyon (100% wool, approx. 109yds/100m per 1¾oz/50g ball) worsted (Aran) weight yarn
- 1 ball each of:
  - Shade 369 (A)
  - Shade 319 (B)

Rico Essentials Soft Merino Aran (100% wool, approx. 109yds/100m per 1¾oz/50g ball) worsted (Aran) weight yarn
- 1 ball each of:
  - Black shade 090 (C)
  - Natural shade 060 (D)

US size 7 (4.5mm) crochet hook

Yarn needle

14in (35cm) square pillow form

FINISHED MEASUREMENTS:

Each square (once blocked): 4¾in (12cm) square

Pillow cover: 14¼in (36cm) square

GAUGE (TENSION):

Rounds 1–4 = 2¼in (6cm) diameter, using US size 7 (4.5mm) hook.

ABBREVIATIONS:

See page 127

FOR THE COVER

CIRCLES (make 9 in each of A and B)

Using A or B, make a magic ring, or ch6 and join with ss in first ch to form a ring.

Round 1: Ch1 (does not count as st throughout), 6sc into the ring, join with ss in first sc. *6 sts.*

Round 2: Ch1, 2sc in each st to end, join with ss in first sc. *12 sts.*

Round 3: Ch1, [2sc in next st, 1sc in next st] 6 times, join with ss in in first sc. *18 sts.*

Round 4: Ch1, [2sc in next st, 1sc in each of next 2 sts] 6 times, join with ss in first sc. *24 sts.*

Round 5: Ch1, [2sc in next st, 1sc in each of next 3 sts] 6 times, join with ss in first sc. *30 sts.*

Round 6: Ch1, [2sc in next st, 1sc in each of next 4 sts] 6 times, join with ss in first sc. *36 sts.*

Fasten off.

SQUARING THE CIRCLES (make 9 in each of C and D)

Taking any circle, join C or D in any st.

Round 1: Ch3 (counts as first dc), 1dc in same st, *1dc in next st, 1hdc in each of next 2 sts, 1sc in each of next 2 sts, 1hdc in each of next 2 sts, 1dc in next st, (2dc, ch2, 2dc) in next st (corner); rep from * twice more, 1dc in next st, 1hdc in each of next 2 sts, 1sc in each of next 2 sts, 1hdc in each of next 2 sts, 1dc in next st, (2dc, ch2) in beg st, join with ss in 3rd of beg 3-ch. *48 dc + four 2-ch sps.*

Round 2: Ch1 (does not count as st), 2sc in corner 2-ch sp, *skip next st, 1sc in each of next 11 sts, (2sc, ch2, 2sc) in corner 2-ch sp; rep from * twice, skip next st, 1sc in each of next 11 sts, (2sc, ch2) in beg corner st, join with ss in first sc. *60 sc + four 2-ch sps.*

Fasten off.

MAKING UP AND FINISHING

Block all the squares before joining.

Lay nine of the squares out in three rows of three in any sequence you like. Using a yarn needle and matching background yarn and with squares RS facing, join together using whip stitch (see page 125), working into the outside loop only of the corresponding edge stitches. Do not pull the yarn too tightly when sewing. Make a second large square with the other nine squares.

BORDER

Join a matching yarn (C or D) in any corner sp of large square, ch1 (counts as 1sc), 1sc in same sp, *1sc in each st (but do not work sc in stitched joins) to corner sp, (2sc, ch2, 2sc) in corner sp; rep from * to beg corner, (2sc, ch2) in beg 2-ch sp, join with ss in beg 1-ch.

Fasten off, then rep on the second square.

JOINING THE PIECES

Position the two large squares with WS together and matching the stitches across each side edge—as you join the squares, when three sides of the large square have been joined insert the pillow form before joining the final side. Working through both squares, join A or B in any 2-ch sp corner, and ch1 (counts as first sc). Work a single crochet seam (see page 124) to join the two pieces, working (1sc, ch2, 1sc) in each corner sp, ending (1sc, ch2) in the beg corner, join with a ss in beg 1-ch.

Fasten off and sew in all yarn ends carefully.

• A word of caution—the yarn quantities listed are exact to the very last thread: one ball of the Noro colors will make 9 circles with just enough yarn left over to work the border. The same goes for the Rico yarn, so if you are nervous of running out you may want to buy an extra ball of each.

MINDFULNESS

Working a loose gauge (tension) has a soothing effect and can be wonderfully calming. The aim is for the stitches to float off the hook with little effort—if you find yourself fighting the tendency to pull your stitches then this is an opportunity to gently explore, without judgment, other thoughts, emotions, and behavior patterns where you may also be holding on tightly. Perhaps now is the time to release your grip a little, to let go to those ways of being that no longer serve you.

openwork winter scarf

This scarf is all about keeping the gauge (tension) super loose, to create a lovely, light, airy drape to the finished piece. If your tension is usually tight then you may want to practice a few rows to get a feel for working loosely—or go up a hook size.

SKILL RATING: ● ● ●

MATERIALS:

Premier Yarns Elle By Me Odette (22% alpaca, 22% wool, 23% polyester, 15% acrylic, 18% metallic, approx. 328yds/300m per 3½oz/100g ball) bulky (chunky) weight yarn
- 1 ball each of:
  - Fog shade 09 (A)
  - Steel shade 11 (B)

Rico Fashion Light Luxury (74% alpaca, 22% wool, 4% polyamide, approx. 142yds/130m per 1¾oz/50g ball) super bulky (super chunky) weight yarn
- 1 ball of Orchid shade 041 (C)

US size M/13 (9mm) hook

FINISHED MEASUREMENTS:

12¼in (31cm) wide, 71in (180cm) long (excluding tassels)

GAUGE (TENSION):

8 sts x 4.5 rows = 4in (10cm) over double crochet, using US size M/13 (9mm) hook.

ABBREVIATIONS:

See page 127.

FOR THE SCARF

Using A, ch26.

Row 1: 1dc in 4th ch from hook (skipped 3-ch counts as dc), 1dc in each ch to end. *24 sts.*

Row 2: Ch3 (counts as first dc throughout), 1dc in each of next 22 sts, 1dc in 3rd of beg 3-ch from prev row. *24 dc.*

Rows 3–13: Rep row 2, changing to C on last dc of row 13.

Rows 14 and 15: Using C, rep row 2, changing to B on last dc of row 15.

Rows 16 and 17: Using B, rep row 2, changing to C on last dc of row 17, carrying yarn up edge and keeping it very loose. Avoid pulling tightly as this will distort shape of scarf.

Rows 18 and 19: Using C, rep row 2, changing to B on last dc of row 19.

Rows 20 and 21: Using B, rep row 2, changing to C on last dc of row 21.

Rep rows 18–21 a further 12 times until you have made 14 stripes in C and 14 in B in total, changing to yarn A on last dc of last row.

Fasten off C and B.

Rows 70–82: Using A, rep row 2.

Fasten off.

- Make the foundation chain very loose by either keeping your gauge (tension) loose, or use a US size N/15 (10mm) hook if you have one in your collection. Remember to change back to a US size M/13 (9mm) hook after the chain is completed.
- Work into stitches and not between the posts, which can sometimes happen when starting out in crochet.
- It is very easy to skip the last double crochet made into the top of the turning chain from the previous row, so count your stitches on every row until you are completely confident.
- When changing color, introduce the new color on the last yarn over hook of the current row.
- Keep both colors attached to the work throughout, bringing the yarn up to the current row when required. Keep the yarn very loose—avoid pulling it tight as this will distort the shape of the scarf. This means that along one side of your scarf you will see the grey and the pink yarns being carried up to the next color change.

MAKING UP AND FINISHING

Sew in all yarn ends carefully.

ADD THE TASSELS

Cut 24 lengths of each color, each 8in (20cm) long. Holding one strand of each color together, make a tassel (see page 125). Attach one tassel to first and last stitches of the foundation row, and space another ten tassels equally between them. Repeat for the other end of the scarf. Trim the tassels to the desired length.

mindfulness cowl

This cowl, with its simple repeat pattern and working a new yarn with every row, is designed to give you a mini mindful break. Aim to complete three rows in a sitting and be aware of the different texture of the yarns.

MINDFULNESS

In a world of distractions, it's important to make time to strengthen your mindfulness muscle and focus your awareness. When using laceweight mohair, slow the pace and draw your focus toward the softness of each stitch as it passes through your fingertips. This can help you reconnect with your body and move away from spending so much time in your head.

SKILL RATING: ● ● ●

MATERIALS:

Adriafil Zebrino (53% wool, 47% acrylic, approx. 136yds/125m per 1¾oz/50g ball) worsted (Aran) weight yarn
- 1 ball each of:
  - Shade 66 (A)
  - Shade 62 (B)

Rico Essentials Super Kid Mohair Loves Silk (70% mohair, 30% silk, approx. 219yds/200m per ⅞oz/25g ball) sport (4 ply) weight yarn
- 1 x ball of Silver shade 008 (C)

US size 7 (4.5mm) crochet hook

Yarn needle

FINISHED MEASUREMENTS:

31½in (79cm) long x 11in (28cm) wide (flat and blocked before joining ends)

GAUGE (TENSION):

12 sts x 13 rows = 4in (10cm) over single crochet, using US size 7 (4.5mm) hook.

ABBREVIATIONS:

See page 127.

FOR THE COWL

Using A, ch36.

Row 1: 1sc in 3rd ch from hook, 1sc in each ch to end, changing to B on last st, turn. *34 sts.*

Row 2: Using B, ch1 (does not count as st throughout), 1sc in each st to end, changing to C on last st, turn.

Row 3: Using C, ch2 (counts as first hdc throughout), 1hdc FLO in each st to end, changing to A on last st, turn.

Row 4: Using A, ch1, 1sc in each st to end, changing to B on last st, turn.

Row 5: Using B, ch1, 1sc in each st to end, changing to C on last st, turn.

Row 6: Using C, ch2, 1hdc FLO in each st to end, changing to A on last st, turn.

Rows 7–90: Rep patt rows 4–6, changing yarn on each row in sequence A, B, C, ending with a C row.

Fasten off.

MAKING UP AND FINISHING

Sew in all yarn ends carefully and block.

With the scarf laid out flat, take the corners of one end and flip them over to create a twist in the middle of the scarf. Using A, join the two ends together with whip stitch (see page 125, preserving the twist.

- **Join in the new color on the final yarn round hook of the current round. Do not fasten off the old color because you will be picking the yarn up again every third row.**

L'EPATANT

MINDFULNESS

If you are in need of grounding and being present in your body this project is just the ticket, as it focuses more on doing rather than being—by this I mean it's physical and fun.

meditation rug

A super-soft rug that feels like you are sitting on a cloud and is perfect for meditation! This is a fantastically quick project to make—the yarn has super squish appeal and once you get the hang of working with such a large hook (or your fingers), it becomes something of a mission to get it made in one sitting. I found the trickiest part was working the first two rounds, because it takes a little getting used to.

SKILL RATING: ● ● ●

MATERIALS:

Lion Brand AR Workshop Chunky Knit (100% polyester, approx. 28yds/26m per 8oz/226g ball) super bulky (super chunky) weight yarn
3 balls of Python 154H (A)
1 ball of Husk 098AM (B)

US size S (20mm) crochet hook (or use fingers)

FINISHED MEASUREMENTS:

33in (83cm) diameter

GAUGE (TENSION):

Round 1 = 6in (15cm) diameter, using US size S (20mm) hook.

ABBREVIATIONS:

See page 127.

FOR THE RUG

Using A and either a US size S (20mm) hook or your thumb and fingers, ch2.

Round 1: 6sc in first ch, join with ss in first sc. *6 sts.*

Round 2: Ch1 (does not count as st), 2sc in each st to end, join with ss in first sc. *12 sts.*

Round 3: Ch2 (counts as 1sc + ch1 throughout), [(1sc, ch1) into next st] 11 times, using B, join with ss in first of beg 2-ch. Do not cut A. *12 sts + twelve 1-ch sps.*

Round 4: Using B, ch3 (counts as 1sc + ch2), [1sc in next 1-ch sp, ch2] 11 times, using A, join with ss in first of beg 3-ch. *12 sts + twelve 2-ch sps.*

Round 5: Ch2, [2sc in next 2-ch sp, ch1] 11 times, 1sc in last 1-ch sp, join with ss in first of beg 2-ch. *24 sts + twelve 1-ch sps.*

Round 6: Ss in first 1-ch sp, ch4 (counts as 1sc + ch3), [1sc in next 1-ch sp, ch3] 11 times, join with ss in first of beg 4-ch. *12 sts + twelve 3-ch sps.*
Fasten off A, leaving 25cm (10in) end.

Round 7: Join B in any 3-ch sp, ch2 (counts as 1sc + ch1 throughout), 1sc in same sp, ch2, [(1sc, ch1, 1sc) in next 3-ch sp, ch2] 11 times, join with ss in first of beg 2-ch. *24 sts + twelve 1-ch sps + twelve 2-ch sps.*
Fasten off B, leaving 25cm (10in) end.

Round 8: Join A in any 1-ch sp from prev round, ch2, [(1sc, ch1, 1sc) in next 2-ch sp, ch1, 1sc in next 1-ch sp, ch1] 11 times, (1sc, ch1, 1sc) in next 2-ch sp, ch1, join with ss in first of beg 2-ch. *36 sts + thirty-six 1-ch sps.*

Round 9: Ss in first 1-ch sp, ch2, [1sc in next 1-ch sp, ch2, 1sc in next 1-ch sp, ch1] 11 times, 1sc in next 1-ch sp, ch2, join with ss in first of beg 2-ch.
Fasten off.

MAKING UP AND FINISHING

Weave in all yarn ends carefully.

- The easiest way to fasten in all the yarn ends is simply to use your fingers and weave them in and around the stitches.
- When joining in a new color or new ball in the middle of your work, remember to leave 8in (20cm) ends at the end of the current ball and the beginning of the new ball so you'll have enough to weave in all the ends.
- Don't pull the yarn too tight (almost impossible to do this but still it's worth saying)—and if you do need to pull any stitches out, take it slow and ease them with your fingers as the yarn likes to cling to itself.

MINDFULNESS

Sometimes it's good to revisit our expectations and make adjustments. Breast cancer and the consequent mastectomy have taught me to love my body, love my imperfections, and love myself. Let this wrap guide you toward a deeper acceptance of those imperfections in your life, your body, and your crochet, and in the process deepen your ability to let go of judgment.

ripple wrap of mindful imperfections

The wonderful chevron effect in this wrap is created by working extra stitches in one place for a peak and skipping stitches for a valley. Hidden within it are little imperfections, mistakes I have made whilst working the pattern, which I've used to practice acceptance and letting go. To observe and not change; to notice and to be OK with what I find. Crochet is a journey and sometimes the "mistakes" we make can be worked into our creation—not everything needs to be pulled out and made perfect.

SKILL RATING: ● ● ●

MATERIALS:

Scheepjes Our Tribe (70% wool, 30% polyamide, approx. 459yds/420m per 3½oz/100g ball) fingering (4 ply) weight yarn

1 ball each of:

Lavender Smoke shade 883 (A)

Miss Neriss shade 966 (B)

Look At What I Made shade 972 (C)

Scheepjes Mohair Rhythm (70% mohair, 30% microfiber, approx. 218yds/200m per ⅞oz/25g ball) lace weight yarn

2 balls of Merengue shade 686 (D)

US size 7 (4.5mm) crochet hook

Yarn needle

FINISHED MEASUREMENTS:

Approx. 17in (43cm) wide x 80in (200cm) long

GAUGE (TENSION):

(10hdc, 2hdc, ch2, 2hdc) in same st to form peak + 10 hdc = 4in (10cm), 9 rows = 4in (10cm), using US size 7 (4.5mm) hook.

ABBREVIATIONS:

See page 127.

SPECIAL ABBREVIATION:

crossed2dc (crossed 2 double crochet): skip next st, 1dc in next st then work 1dc in skipped st (working over first dc)

- Work in the back loop only on all rows except when working with yarn D.
- You'll begin each row with "ch2, 1hdc in each of next 2 sts, skip next st" and work the last 4 sts on all rows "skip 2 sts, 1hdc in each of last 2 sts."
- To make a peak work: (2hdc, ch2, 2hdc) and to make a valley "skip 3 sts."
- The pattern is in multiples of 24 + 4 stitches.

FOR THE WRAP

Using A, ch102.

Row 1: 1hdc in 3rd ch from hook (skipped 2-ch does not count as st), 1hdc in next ch, skip next ch, *1hdc in each of next 10 ch, (2hdc, ch3, 2hdc) in next ch (for peak), 1hdc in each of next 10 ch, skip next 3 ch (for valley); rep from * 3 more times, ending final rep with skip next 2 ch (for 5th and final valley), 1hdc in each of last 2 ch.

Row 2: Ch2 (does not count as st throughout), 1hdc BLO in each of first 2 sts, skip next st, *1hdc BLO in each of next 10 sts, (2hdc, ch3, 2hdc) in next ch sp (for peak), 1hdc BLO in each of next 10 sts, skip next 3 sts (for valley); rep from * 3 more times, ending final rep with skip next 2 sts (for last valley), 1hdc BLO in each of last 2 sts.

Rows 3–10: Rep row 2.

Rows 11–14: Using B, rep row 2.

Rows 15 and 16 (non-BLO rows): Using D, work as row 2 but work every hdc through both loops.

Rows 17–20: Using B, rep row 2 (working in BLO again).

Row 21 (crossed dc row): Using A and working in BLO throughout, ch2, 1dc in each of next 2 sts, skip next st, *[work crossed2dc over next 2 sts] 5 times, (2dc, ch2, 2dc) in next ch sp (first peak), [work crossed2dc over next 2 sts] 5 times, skip next 3 sts (for valley); rep from * 3 more times, ending final rep with skip next 2 sts (for last valley), 1dc in each of last 2 sts.

Rows 11–21 form patt, rep them 3 more times.

Cont to rep patt rows 11–21, changing color as foll:

Row 55: C.
Row 56–58: B.
Rows 59 and 60: D
Row 61: C.
Rows 62 and 63: B.
Row 64: C.
Row 65 (crossed dc row): A.
Row 66: B.
Row 67: C.
Row 68: B.
Row 69: C.
Rows 70 and 71 (non-BLO rows): D.
Rows 72 and 73: C.
Row 74: B.
Row 75: C.
Row 76 (crossed dc row): A.
Rows 77–80: C.
Rows 81–82 (non-BLO rows): D.
Rows 83–86: C.
Row 87 (crossed dc row): A.
Rows 88–109: Rep rows 77–87 twice more.
Rows 110–113: C.
Rows 114–115 (non-BLO rows): D.
Rows 116–119: C.
Rows 120–129: Using A, rep row 2.

Fasten off.

MAKING UP AND FINISHING

Sew in all yarn ends carefully.

comfort mittens

These little mitts are so simple to make—the squares are joined to make a tube with a hole for the thumb! Each square has a squidgy puff stitch center, for extra insulation on a cold day.

MINDFULNESS

On days when my pain levels are high I find the texture of the yarn can be of great benefit. The softer and lighter it is, the more comforting it becomes, soothing the pain and helping me relax. By placing the emphasis on exploring the physical sensations of working the yarn—rather than focusing on the end goal of finishing a round—you can observe how it makes you feel. Notice, without judgment, where this experience takes you.

SKILL RATING: ● ● ●

MATERIALS:

Lang Yarns Mille Colori Baby (100% wool, approx. 207yds/190m per 1¾oz/50g ball) fingering (4 ply) weight yarn
 1 ball of shade 061 (A)

Scheepjes Alpaca Rhythm (80% alpaca, 20% wool, approx. 218yds/200m per ⅞oz/25g ball) lace weight yarn
 1 ball of Paso shade 662 (B)

Scheepjes Mohair Rhythm (70% mohair, 30% microfiber, approx. 218yds/200m per ⅞oz/25g ball) lace weight yarn
 1 ball of Merengue shade 686 (C)
 1 ball of Vogue shade 681 (D)

US size G/6 (4mm) crochet hook

Yarn needle

FINISHED MEASUREMENTS:

8in (20cm) circumference x 6¾in (17cm) long

GAUGE (TENSION):

Rounds 1–3 = 2¼in (5.5cm) square, using US size G/6 (4mm) hook.

ABBREVIATIONS:

See page 127.

SPECIAL ABBREVIATION:

PS (puff stitch): *yo, insert hook into st and pull a loop through keeping the yarn loops long; rep from * 4 more times into same st, yo and draw through all loops on hook, 1ch to close st

FOR THE MITTENS

PUFF CENTERS (make 24—12 per mitten)

Using a strand of A and C held tog, make a magic ring, or ch6 and join with ss in first ch to form a ring.

Round 1: Ch1 (does not count as a st), 8sc in ring. *8 sts.*

Round 2: Ch3 (does not count as a st), 1PS in first sc, ch2 (makes 3-ch sp), *1PS in next sc, ch2; rep from * to end, join with ss in top of beg PS. *8 PS + eight 3-ch sps.*

Fasten off A.

Finish and join squares using join-as-you-go method (see page 122) to make a rectangle of 3 rows of 4 squares, as foll:

STARTER SQUARE

Round 3: Join B and C tog in any 3-ch sp, hold as one strand throughout. Ch2 (counts as first hdc throughout), 2hdc in same 3-ch sp (makes half corner), 3sc in next 3-ch sp, *(3hdc, ch2, 3hdc) in next ch-3 sp, 3sc in next 3-ch sp; rep from * twice more, 3hdc in beg 3-ch sp, ch2, join with ss in 2nd of beg 2-ch.

Fasten off B and C.

SECOND SQUARE

Round 3: Join B and C tog in any 3-ch sp, hold as one strand throughout. Ch2, 2hdc in same 3-ch sp (makes half corner), 3sc in next 3-ch sp, 3hdc in next 3-ch sp then instead of ch2 for corner sp, insert hook in corner sp of starter square from underneath, 1sc in corner of starter square (counts as first of 2-ch for corner sp), ch1, work second 3-hdc group in corner sp of second square as usual. Cont joining squares tog, making 1sc in next side sp between 3-hdc and 3-sc of starter square followed by 3sc in next 3-ch sp of second square, 1sc in next sp between 3-sc and 3-hdc of starter square, 3hdc in next 3-ch sp in second square, 1sc in next corner sp of starter square, ch1, 3hdc group in same corner 3-ch sp of second square. When second square is joined to starter square along one side, cont around to finish round 3 as normal.

Cont to join squares in this way throughout. When joining a square to two prev squares at a shared corner, replace both corner ch with 1sc in each adjoining square.

Rep to make a rectangle of 3 rows of 4 squares for second mitten.

MAKING UP AND FINISHING

Sew in all yarn ends carefully.

Lay each mitten flat and then fold in half with RS together, joining the two short ends. Using a length of B and C held tog, sew the ends of row 1 and row 3 together using whip stitch (see page 125), and leaving row 2 open for the thumbhole.

THUMBHOLE EDGING

Turn each mitten RS out. Join B and C in any st around thumbhole.

Round 1: Ch1 (counts as sc throughout), 1sc in each of next 19 sts around thumbhole, join with ss in beg 1-ch. *20 sts.*

Round 2: Ch1, 1sc in each st to end, join with ss in beg 1-ch.

Fasten off and sew in ends.

chapter 3

mindful meditation

MINDFULNESS

This project requires careful counting on the first 7 to 9 rounds, so make this part of the mindful practice. Slow your stitches and get a gentle rhythm going between your breath and the flow of the hook with the yarn. There's no rush and the slower you go the easier it becomes.

boho baskets

Play with the colors on these sweet little baskets and go where your heart takes you. I've worked some of them in graded tones from light to dark, but the multi-colored one is a glorious melange of lots of different colors. Each basket becomes its own unique creation just like you.

SKILL RATING: ● ● ●

MATERIALS:

Scheepjes Cahlista (100% cotton, approx. 92yds/85m per 1¾oz/50g ball) worsted (Aran) weight yarn

Blue basket:
1 ball each of:
- Bridal White shade 105
- Bluebell shade 173
- Cyan shade 397
- Electric Blue shade 201

Pink basket:
1 ball each of:
- Bridal White shade 105
- Powder Pink shade 238
- Fresia shade 519
- Shocking Pink shade 114

Green basket:
1 ball each of:
- Bridal White shade 105
- Primrose shade 522
- Lime Juice shade 392
- Apple Granny shade 513

Large mutli-colored basket:
⅓ ball each of all of above plus:
- Royal Orange shade 189
- Tangerine shade 281
- Yellow Gold shade 208
- Light Orchid shade 226

US size 7 (4.5mm) crochet hook

Stitch marker

Yarn needle

FINISHED MEASUREMENTS:

Blue basket: 3¼in (8cm) diameter, 2¾in (7cm) deep

Green basket: 3½in (9cm) diameter, 2¾in (7cm) deep

Pink basket: 4in (10cm) diameter, 3¾in (9.5cm) deep

Multi-colored basket: 5½in (14cm) diameter, 4in (10cm) deep

GAUGE (TENSION):

10 sts x 13 rows = 4in (10cm) over single crochet, using US size 7 (4.5mm) hook and two strands of yarn held together.

ABBREVIATIONS:

See page 127.

FOR THE BASKETS

BLUE BASKET

Hold two strands of different colors tog throughout.
Using first 2 colors held tog, make a magic ring, or ch6 and join with ss in first ch to form a ring.
Round 1: Ch1 (does not count as st throughout), 6sc into the ring, join with ss in first sc. *6 sts.*
Round 2: Ch1, 2sc in each st to end, join with ss in first sc. *12 sts.*
Round 3: Ch1, [1sc in next st, 2sc in next st] 6 times, join with ss in first sc. *18 sts.*
Round 4: Ch1, [1sc in each of next 2 sts, 2sc in next st] 6 times, join with ss in first sc. *24 sts.*
Round 5: Ch1, [1sc in each of next 3 sts, 2sc in next st] 6 times, join with ss in first sc. *30 sts.*

MAKE THE SIDES

Beg to work in cont spiral with 1sc in each st, changing color as desired. PM in first st and move up as each round is completed.
As sides begin to "curl" up, turn work inside out, cont to crochet in anti-clockwise direction.
When you have reached desired height, join last round with ss in first st.
Fasten off.

- Keep your gauge (tension) tight as this helps with the stability of the basket. Working a tight gauge (tension) with two strands held as one can make your hand and arm ache, so a little rest every few rows really helps.
- The base for the baskets is worked in rounds joined with a ss. Each round begins with ch1, which is not counted as a stitch. To avoid losing a stitch, always work the first sc into the same stitch at the base of the beginning ch1.
- To blend the colors gently, cut one of the yarns leaving a 4in (10cm) end and introduce a new color on the next yarn round hook, working over all the yarn ends as you go. For dramatic color changes as on the multi-colored basket, cut both yarns leaving 4in (10cm) ends and work one more single crochet in these two colors, changing to two new colors on the last yarn round hook and working over all yarn ends.

GREEN BASKET

Work as blue basket to end of round 5.
Round 6: Ch1, [1sc in each of next 4 sts, 2sc in next st] 6 times, join with ss in first sc. *36 sts.*
Work sides as Blue Basket.

PINK BASKET

Work as green basket to end of round 6.
Round 7: Ch1, [1sc in each of next 5 sts, 2sc in next st] 6 times, join with ss in first sc. *42 sts.*
Work sides as Blue Basket.

MULTI-COLORED BASKET

Work as pink basket to end of round 7.
Round 8: Ch1, [1sc in each of next 6 sts, 2sc in next st] 6 times, join with ss in first sc. *48 sts.*
Round 9: Ch1, [1sc in each of next 7 sts, 2sc in next st] 6 times, join with ss in first sc. *54 sts.*
Work sides as Blue Basket.

MAKING UP AND FINISHING

Sew in all yarn ends carefully.

mandala in a hoop

Take your time on each round of this mandala and enjoy the fresh spring colors of the yarn. It is important to count the stitches as you go, and the simple act of counting acts as a mantra that really can slow your thoughts right down.

SKILL RATING: ● ● ●

MATERIALS:

Rico Ricorumi DK (100% cotton, approx. 63yds/58m per ⅞oz/25g ball) light worsted (DK) weight yarn

1 ball each of:
- Cream shade 002 (A)
- Light Green shade 046 (B)
- Fuchsia shade 014 (C)
- Lilac shade 017 (D)

US size G/6 (4mm) crochet hook

Yarn needle

12in (30cm) diameter embroidery hoop inner

FINISHED MEASUREMENTS:

11½in (29cm) diameter

GAUGE (TENSION):

Rounds 1 to 4 = 3¼in (8cm) diameter, using US size G/6 (4mm) hook.

ABBREVIATIONS:

See page 127.

SPECIAL ABBREVIATIONS:

4-hdc cl (4-half double crochet cluster): yo, insert hook in st, yo, pull a loop through (3 loops on hook), yo, pull through 2 loops on hook (2 loops on hook), yo, insert hook in next st, yo, pull a loop through (4 loops on hook), yo, pull through 2 loops on hook (3 loops on hook), yo, insert hook in next st, yo, pull a loop through (5 loops on hook), yo, pull through 2 loops on hook (4 loops on hook), yo, pull through all 4 loops to gather cluster tog

FPhdc (front post half double crochet): yo, take hook from front around post of st in prev round, yo, pull a loop through (3 loops on hook), yo, pull through all 3 loops

FPhdc dec (front post half double crochet decrease): yo, insert hook from front around post of st in prev round, yo, pull a loop through (3 loops on hook), yo, pull through 2 loops (2 loops on hook), yo, take hook from front around post of next st in prev round, yo, pull a loop though (4 loops on hook), yo, pull through all 4 loops

MP (make picot): ch3, ss in 3rd ch from hook

PC (3-dc popcorn): work 3dc all in same st, remove hook from loop and insert from front to back in top of first dc made, pick up dropped loop and pull through, ch1

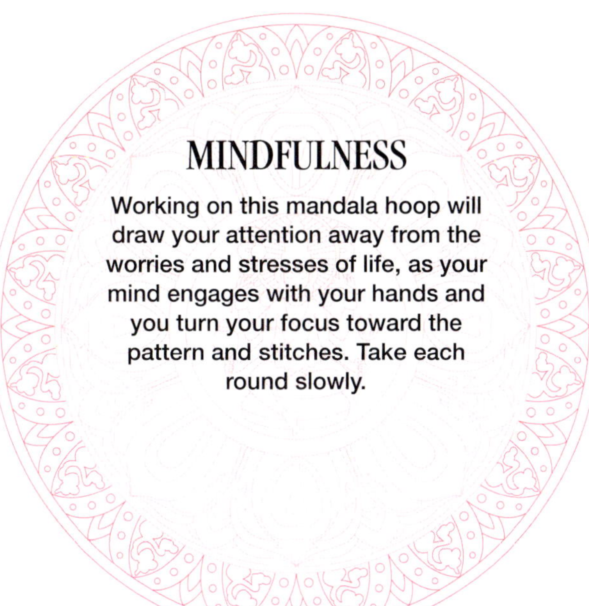

FOR THE MANDALA

Using A, make a magic ring, or ch6 and join with ss in first ch to form a ring.

Round 1: Ch1 (does not count as st), 8sc into the ring, join with ss in first sc. *8 sts.*
Fasten off.

Round 2: Join B in any st, ch3 (counts as first dc throughout), 2dc in same st, ch3, PC in next st, ch3, (PC, 3ch) in each st to end, join with ss in top of beg 3-ch. *8 PC + eight 3-ch sps.*

Round 3: Join C in any 3-ch sp, ch3, (2dc, ch2, PC) in same sp, ch2, *(PC, ch2, PC) in next 3-ch sp, ch2; rep from * to end, join with ss in 3rd of beg 3-ch. *16 PC + sixteen 2-ch sps.*
Fasten off.

Round 4: Join D in any 2-ch sp, ch1 (counts as first sc throughout), 2sc in same sp, 3sc in each 2-ch sp to end, join with ss in beg 1-ch. *48 sts.*
Fasten off.

Round 5: Join B in first sc of any 3-sc group in prev row, ch1, [ch3, skip 2 sts, 1sc] 15 times, ch3, skip last 2 sts, join with ss in beg 1-ch. *16 sc + sixteen 3-ch sps.*
Fasten off.

Round 6: Join A in any 3-ch sp, ch2 (counts as first hdc throughout), 3hdc in same sp, *4hdc in next 3-ch sp; rep from * to end, join with ss into 2nd of beg 2-ch. *64 sts.*
Fasten off.

Round 7: Join C in first hdc of any 4-hdc group in prev round, ch4 (counts as 1tr), skip 3 sts, *(1tr, ch4, 1tr) in next st, skip 3 sts; rep from * 14 times, 1tr in same sp as beg 4-ch, ch4, join with ss in 4th of beg 4-ch. *32 tr + sixteen 4-ch sps.*
Fasten off.

Round 8: Join D in any 4-ch sp, ch2, 5hdc in same sp, FPhdc dec over next 2 tr, [6hdc in next 4-ch sp, FPhdc dec over next 2 tr] 15 times, join with ss in 2nd of beg 2-ch. *96 hdc + 16 FPhdc dec.*
Fasten off.

Round 9: Join A around front post of any FPhdc dec from prev round, ch5 (counts as 1FPhdc and ch3), *skip 3 sts, 1sc in next st, ch3, skip 2 sts, 1FPhdc in next FPhdc dec from prev round; rep from * to end, finishing last rep with ch3, skip last 2 sts, join with ss in 2nd of beg 5-ch, do not fasten off. *16 FPhdc +16 sc + 32 3-ch sps.*

Round 10: Ch1, 3sc in first 3-ch sp, 4sc in each 3-ch sp around, join with ss in beg 1-ch. *128 sts.*
Fasten off.

Round 11: Join B in any st, ch2, 1hdc in each st to end, join with ss in 2nd of beg 2-ch.
Fasten off.

Round 12: Join C in any st above sc from round 9, ch2 (counts as first st of 4-hdc cl), complete 4-hdc cl over next 3 sts, [4-hdc cl, ch5] to end. *Thirty-two 4-hdc cl + thirty-two 5-ch sps.*
Fasten off.

Round 13: Join A in any 5-ch sp, ch2, (4dc, 1hdc) in same sp, *(1hdc, 4dc, 1hdc) in next 5-ch sp; rep from * to end, join with ss in 2nd of 2-ch. *192 sts.*

Round 14: Join D around front post of any 4-hdc cl from round 12, ch2 (counts as 1FPhdc), *ch3, skip 3 sts, (ss, MP, ss) in next st, ch3, skip 2 sts, 1FPhdc in next 4-hdc cl from round 12; rep from * to end, finishing last rep with ch3, skip last 2 sts, ss in 2nd of beg 5-ch.
Fasten off.

MAKING UP AND FINISHING

Sew in all yarn ends carefully.

Using D, join the mandala to the hoop, sewing through the picot from back to front and then taking the yarn up and over the hoop.

hanging gardens plant holder

These little hanging baskets can be adapted to fit any size pot, so you can start small and crochet up a bigger hanger as your plant grows. I've worked a version of this pattern to include beads, which are a great way of adding a pop of color to your crochet. If you have never worked beads into your crochet then now is the time to embrace the experience of learning something new!

SKILL RATING: ● ● ●

MATERIALS:

Rico Creative Cotton Aran (100% cotton, approx. 92yds/85m per 1¾oz/50g ball) worsted (Aran) weight yarn

- 1 ball each of:
  - Orange shade 74 (A)
  - Fuchsia shade 13 (B)
  - Sky Blue shade 37 (C)
  - Light Green shade 40 (D)

US size J/10 (6mm) crochet hook

Stitch marker

Yarn needle

48 beads (optional, medium pot only)

FINISHED MEASUREMENTS:

Small pot: to fit 2½in (6.5cm) base pot
Medium pot: to fit 4in (10cm) base pot

GAUGE (TENSION):

Rounds 1–2 = 3in (7.5cm) diameter, using US size J/10 (6mm) hook.

ABBREVIATIONS:

See page 127.

SPECIAL ABBREVIATIONS:

place bead sc: insert hook in st, yo, pull a loop through, bring bead up to hook, yo, pull through both loops on hook

place bead ch: bring bead up to hook and ch1

FOR THE HOLDER

SMALL POT

Working with A and B held tog throughout, make a magic ring, or ch6 and join with ss in first ch to form a ring.
Round 1: Ch3 (counts as first dc throughout), 11dc into the ring, join with ss in 3rd of beg 3-ch. *12 sts.*
Round 2: Ch3, 1dc in same st, 2dc in each st to end, join with ss in 3rd of beg 3-ch. *24 sts.*
Round 3: Ch1 (counts as first sc), ch1, [skip next st, 1sc in foll st, ch1] 11 times, skip last st, join with ss in beg 1-ch. *12 sc + twelve 1-ch sps.*
You will see the sides beg to curl up slightly.
Round 4: [1sc in next 1-ch sp, ch4] 12 times, join last 4-ch with ss in first 4-ch. Beg to work in cont spiral. PM in first st and move up as each round is completed.
Round 5: [Ch4, 1sc in next 4-ch sp] to end.
Rep round 5 until desired height is reached.
Final round: [2sc in each 4-ch sp] to end, join with ss in first sc. *24 sc.*
Fasten off.

SMALL POT HANGING STRANDS

At this point the pot cover is looking very floppy and shapeless but fear not!
Work with two strands held tog throughout.
Strand 1: Join yarn in sp between any 2-sc group, ch60 (more for longer hanging depth).
Fasten off, leaving 28in (70cm) end.
Strands 2, 3, and 4: Count 6 sts from prev strand, join yarn in next sp between sc, ch60.
Fasten off, leaving 8in (20cm) end.

MEDIUM POT

Thread all beads onto either C or D, then cont working with C and D held tog throughout.
Work base as small pot to end of round 2.

- **As you work the beads will rise up to the hook and you will need to keep pushing them down until you wish to use one.**

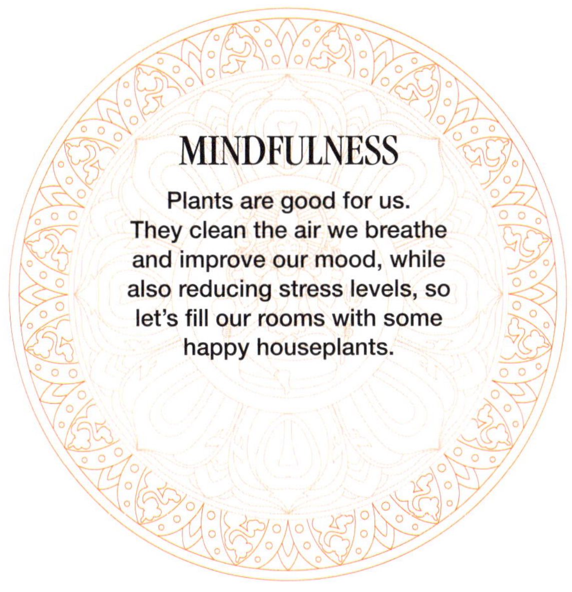

MINDFULNESS

Plants are good for us. They clean the air we breathe and improve our mood, while also reducing stress levels, so let's fill our rooms with some happy houseplants.

Round 3: Ch3, 1dc in same st, [1dc in next st, 2dc in next st] 11 times, 1dc in next st, join with ss in 3rd of beg 3-ch. *36 sts.*
Round 4: Ch1 (counts as first sc), ch2, [skip next 2 sts, 1sc in foll st, ch2] 11 times, skip last 2 sts, join with ss in beg 1-ch. *12 sc + twelve 1-ch sps.*
You will see the sides beg to curl up slightly.
Round 5: [1sc in next 2-ch sp, ch4] 12 times, join last 4-ch with ss in first 4-ch.
Beg to work in cont spiral. PM in first st and move up as each round is completed.
Round 6: [Ch4, 1sc in next 4-ch sp] 12 times.
Round 7: [Ch4, 1sc in next 4-ch sp, ch4, place bead sc in next 4-ch sp] 6 times.
Round 8: Rep round 6.
Round 9: Rep round 7.
Rep rounds 6 and 7 until desired height is reached.
Final round: [3sc in each 4-ch sp] to end, join with ss in first sc. *36 sc.*
Fasten off.

- Adjust the number of rounds to fit the height of the pot—smaller pots may only need a couple of rounds.
- For larger pots work more base rounds, increasing each base round by 6 stitches to keep the base flat.
- Remember the weight of the plant will pull the crochet up over the pot, so allow for this when gauging the fit.

MEDIUM POT HANGING STRANDS
Work with two strands held tog throughout.
Strand 1: Join yarn in any sp between any 3-sc group, ch1, place bead ch, [ch5, place bead ch] 8 times, ch5.
Fasten off, leaving 40in (100cm) end.
Strands 2, 3, and 4: Count 9 sts from prev strand, join yarn in next sp between sc, ch1, place bead ch, [ch5, place bead ch] 8 times, ch5.
Fasten off, leaving 8in (20cm) end.

MAKING UP AND FINISHING

On the small pot, hold all four hanging strands together, making sure they are even in length (it's easy to miscount!), and join them with a big knot. Sew in the three shorter ends, leaving the 28in (70cm) end sticking out at the top. Using the 28in (70cm) end, ch12 then join with a ss in the first ch to form a hanging loop. Fasten off.

On the medium pot, knot all four hanging strands together as for the small pot, leaving the 40in (100cm) end sticking out the top. Using the 40in (100cm) end, ch20 then join with a ss in the first ch to form a hanging loop. Fasten off.

Sew in all remaining yarn ends carefully.

indian summer table mandala

As with most mandalas, some rounds are simple while others require full concentration—making this pattern a great tool for focusing the mind. It's very important with all mandalas to get the stitch count just right because the symmetry is based on mathematics. You can finish at any point to suit your table size.

MINDFULNESS

I often sit and listen to the radio while crocheting, but it's good sometimes to switch off all distractions and allow your mind to become fully present and aware of where you are. Mandalas are perfect for this, so pick a time in your crochet schedule when you are able to sit quietly and immerse yourself without distraction. As you crochet, gently observe your mind and the noisy chatter it may be making. Each time you notice your thoughts have drifted, gently bring your attention back to the present, back to the mandala, back to the crochet.

SKILL RATING: ● ● ●

MATERIALS:

Scheepjes Cahlista (100% cotton, approx. 92yds/85m per 1¾oz/50g ball) worsted (Aran) weight yarn

1 ball each of:
- Bridal White shade 105 (A)
- Yellow Gold shade 208 (B)
- Royal Orange shade 189 (C)
- Shocking Pink shade 114 (D)
- Deep Violet shade 521 (E)
- Crystalline shade 385 (F)
- Bluebird 247 (G)

US size 7 (4.5mm) crochet hook

Yarn needle

FINISHED MEASUREMENTS:

21in (53cm) diameter

GAUGE (TENSION):

Rounds 1–4 = 4½in (11.5cm) diameter, using US size 7 (4.5mm) hook.

ABBREVIATIONS:

See page 127.

SPECIAL ABBREVIATION:

esc (elongated single crochet): insert hook in st two rows below current round, yo, pull yarn up level to current round, yo, pull through both loops on hook to complete esc

FPhdc (front post half double crochet): yo, take hook from front around post of st in previous round, yo, pull a loop through (3 loops on hook), yo, pull through all 3 loops

FOR THE MANDALA

Using A, ch24, join with ss in first ch to form large central ring—this needs to be large enough to comfortably fit the pole of a sun parasol.

Round 1: Ch1 (does not count as st), 32sc into the ring, join with ss in beg 1-ch. *32 sts.*
Fasten off A.

Round 2: Join B in any st, ch2 (counts as first hdc throughout), 1hdc in each st to end. *32 sts.*
Fasten off B.

Round 3: Join C in any st, ch2, 1hdc in same st, 2hdc in each st to end. *64 sts.*
Fasten off C.

Round 4: Join D in any st from round 2 and pull yarn up to level of current round, ch1 (forms first esc), ch1, *1esc in next st from round 2, ch1; rep from * in each st to end, join with ss in beg 1-ch. *32 esc + thirty-two 1-ch sps.*
Fasten off D.

Round 5: Join E in any 1-ch sp, ch1 (counts as first sc throughout), *ch3, skip next 1-ch sp, 1sc in next 1-ch sp; rep from * to last 1-ch sp, ch3, skip last 1-ch sp, join with ss in beg 1-ch. *16 sc + sixteen 1-ch sps.*
Fasten off E.

Round 6: Join F in any 3-ch sp, ch2, (1dc, ch1, 1dc, 1hdc) in same 3-ch sp as join, (1hdc, 1dc, ch1, 1hdc, 1dc) in each 3-ch sp to end, join with ss in 2nd of beg 2-ch.
Fasten off F.

Round 7: Join A in any 1-ch sp between 2 dc, ch1, ch2, 1FPhdc in sc from round 4, ch2, *1sc in sp between 2 dc from round 6, ch2, 1FPhdc in sc from round 4, ch2; rep from * 14 times, join with ss in beg 1-ch.

Round 8: Ch3 (counts as first dc throughout), ch2, 1dc in same st, ch3, *1dc in next sc from round 7, ch2, 1dc in same st, ch3; rep from * 14 times, join with ss in 3rd of beg 3-ch.

Fasten off A.

Round 9: Join D in any 3-ch sp, ch1, (1hdc, 1dc, 1tr, ch1,1tr, 1dc, 1hdc) in next 2-ch sp, *1sc in next 3-ch sp, (1hdc, 1dc, 1tr, ch1, 1tr, 1dc, 1hdc) in next 2-ch sp; rep from * 14 times, join with ss in beg 1-ch.

Fasten off D.

Round 10: Join E in any 1-ch sp (tip of D triangle), ch1, ch6, [1sc in next 1-ch sp, ch6] 15 times, join with ss in beg 1-ch. *16 sc + sixteen 6-ch sps.*

Fasten off E.

Round 11: Join G in 6-ch sp, ch2, 7hdc in same 6-ch sp, [8hdc in next 6-ch sp] 15 times, join with ss in 2nd of beg 2-ch. *128 sts.*

Fasten off G.

Round 12: Join A around FP of any sc of round 10, ch2 (counts as first FPhdc), ch1, skip first st of 8-hdc group, [1sc in next st, ch1, skip next st] 3 times, *1FPhdc in next sc from round 10, ch1, skip first st of 8-hdc group, [1sc in next st, ch1, skip next st] 3 times; rep from * 14 times, join with ss in 2nd beg 2-ch.

Fasten off A.

Round 13: Join F in any 1-ch sp, ch2, 1hdc in same sp, 2hdc in each 1-ch sp to end, join with ss in 2nd of beg 2-ch.

Fasten off F.

Round 14: Join B in sp between any 2-hdc group, ch1, 1sc in same sp, ch1, skip next 2 hdc, [2sc in next sp between 2-hdc groups, ch1, skip next 2 hdc] to end, join with ss in beg 1-ch.

Fasten off B.

Round 15: Join C in any 1-ch sp, ch1, ch2, [skip next 2 sc, 1sc in next 1-ch sp, ch2] to end, join with ss in beg 1-ch. *64 sc + sixty-four 2-ch sps.*
Fasten off C.
Round 16: Join A in any 2-ch sp, ch3, ch1, 1dc in same sp, (1dc, ch1, 1dc) in each 2-ch sp to end, join with ss in 3rd of beg 3-ch. *128 dc + sixty-four 1-ch sps.*
Fasten off A.
For smaller table end here, for larger tables cont as foll:
Round 17: Join B in any 1-ch sp, ch1, ch6, [skip next 4 sts and 1-ch sp, 1sc in next 1-ch sp, ch6] to end, join with ss in beg 1-ch. *32 sc + thirty-two 6-ch sps.*
Fasten off B.
Round 18: Join C in center of any 6-ch sp, ch1, ch7, [1sc in center of next 6-ch sp, ch7] to end, join with ss in beg 1-ch. *32 sc + thirty-two 7-ch sps.*
Fasten off C.
Round 19: Join E in center of any 7-ch sp, ch1, ch5, [1sc in center of next 7-ch sp, ch5] to end, join with ss in beg 1-ch. *32 sc + thirty-two 5-ch sps.*
Fasten off E.
Round 20: Join D in any 5-ch sp, ch1, 6sc in same sp, 7sc in each 5-ch sp to end, join with ss in beg 1-ch. *224 sts.*
Fasten off D.
Round 21: Join G in any st, ch1, 1sc in each st to end, join with ss in beg 1-ch.
Fasten off G.
Round 22: Join A around FP of any sc from round 19, ch3 (counts as first FPdc), 1FPdc around same sc, [ch1, skip next st, 1sc] 3 times, skip next st, *2FPdc in next sc from round 19, [ch1, skip next st, 1sc] 3 times, skip next st; rep from * 30 times, join with ss in 3rd of beg 3-ch.
Fasten off A.
Round 23: Join F in any st, ch1, 1sc, [2sc in next 1-ch sp] 3 times, *2sc, [2sc in next 1-ch sp] 3 times; rep from * 30 times, join with ss in beg 1-ch. *256 sts.*
Fasten off F.
Round 24: Using B, ch1, 1sc in each st to end, join with ss in beg 1-ch.
Round 25: Join C in any st, ch1, ch1, skip next st, [1sc, ch1, skip next st] to end, join with ss in beg 1-ch.
Fasten off C.
Round 26: Join D in any st in round 23 that sits directly beneath 1-ch sp from round 25 and pull yarn up to level of current round, ch1 (counts as first esc), *ch1, skip next st of round 23, 1esc in next sc of round 23; rep from * to end, join with ss in beg 1-ch.
Fasten off.

MAKING UP AND FINISHING

Sew in all yarn ends carefully.

Block your work to make it into a neat circle.

light 'n' airy beaded toppers

These mandalas are an homage to my grandmother, who was always hooking a little something like this. If you are a confident beginner and have mastered the granny square you can use this project to expand your crochet repertoire and confidence.

SKILL RATING: ● ● ●

MATERIALS:

Scheepjes Catona (100% cotton, approx. 27yds/25m per ⅜oz/10g ball) fingering (4 ply) weight yarn
1 ball each of:
- Lemon shade 280 (A)
- Icy Pink shade 246 (B)
- Fresia shade 519 (C)
- Bridal White shade 105 (D)
- Shocking Pink shade 114 (E)
- Sweet Orange shade 411 (F)
- Royal Orange shade 189 (G)
- Lavender shade 520 (H)

US size C/2 (2.75mm) crochet hook

Yarn needle

12 beads for each cover

FINISHED MEASUREMENTS:

Small: 8in (20cm) diameter (tip to tip when blocked)
Large: 10in (25cm) diameter (tip to tip when blocked)

GAUGE (TENSION):

Rounds 1–2 = 1½in (4cm) diameter, using US size C/2 (2.75mm) hook.

ABBREVIATIONS:

See page 127.

SPECIAL ABBREVIATIONS:

4-dc cl (4-double crochet cluster): [yo, insert hook in next st, pull a loop through, yo, pull through first 2 loops on hook] 4 times (5 loops on hook), yo, pull through all 5 loops

5-dc cl (5-double crochet cluster): [yo, insert hook in ch sp, pull a loop through, yo, pull through first 2 loops on hook] 5 times in same ch sp (6 loops on hook), yo, pull through all 6 loops

FOR THE COVERS

SMALL COVER

Using A, make a magic ring, or ch6 and join with ss in first ch to form a ring.

Round 1: Ch1 (does not count as st throughout), 6sc into the ring, join with ss in first sc.

Round 2: Ch1, 2sc in each st around. *12 sts.*

Fasten off A, join in B.

Round 3: Ch3 (counts as first dc throughout), 1dc in same st, 2dc in each st to end. *24 sts.*

Fasten off B, join C in any st.

Round 4: Ch4 (counts as first dc and 1-ch), *1dc in next st, ch1; rep from * to end, join with ss in 3rd of beg 4-ch. *24 dc + twenty-four 1-ch sps.*

Fasten off C, join A in any 1-ch sp.

Round 5: Ch2 (counts as first sc), 1sc in same sp, 2sc in each 1-ch sp to end, join with ss in 2nd of beg 2-ch. *48 sts.*

Fasten off A, join D in any st.

Round 6: Ch3 (counts as first st of 4-dc cl), complete 4-dc cl over next 3 sts, *ch5, 4-dc cl over next 4 sts; rep from * to end, ch5, join with ss in top of first 4-dc cl. *Twelve 4-dc cl + twelve 5-ch sps.*

Fasten off D, join B in top of any 4-dc cl.

Round 7: Ch4 (counts as first dc and 1-ch), 1dc in same st, ch2, 1sc in next 5-ch sp, ch2, *(1dc, ch1, 1dc) in top of next 4-dc cl, ch2, 1sc in next 5-ch sp, ch2; rep from * to end, join with ss in 3rd of beg 4-ch.

Fasten off B, join C in any 1-ch sp from prev round.

Round 8: Ch9 (counts as first sc and 8-ch), [1sc in next 1-ch sp from prev round, ch8] 11 times, join with ss in first of beg 9-ch.

Fasten off C.

Thread 12 beads onto D, join yarn in any 8-ch sp.

Round 9: [Ch8, bring bead to hook, ch1, ss in 2nd ch from bead, ch6, 1sc in next 8-ch sp] 12 times, join with ss in first of beg 8-ch.

Fasten off.

MINDFULNESS

Embrace the experience of learning and practice non-judgment. Is your intention when doing a particular pattern that it should make you feel happier and lighter? To gain a sense of achievement and fulfilment at learning something new? Whatever it is, focus on this intent and allow it to expand with every round.

LARGE COVER

Work rounds 1–6 as for small cover, using E for rounds 1–2, F for round 3, G for round 4, A for round 5, H for round 6.
Fasten off H, join D in any 5-ch sp from prev round.

Round 7: Ch3 (counts as first st of 5-dc cl), [yo, insert hook in same sp, yo, pull through 2 loops] 4 times in same sp, yo, pull though all loops on hook (completes first 5-dc cl), ch6, 5-dc cl in next 5-ch sp, ch6; rep from * to end, join with ss in top of first 5-dc cl. *Twelve 5-dc cl + twelve 6-ch sps.*
Fasten off D, join F in top of any 5-dc cl.

Round 8: Ch5 (counts as first dc and 2-ch), 1dc in same st, ch2, 1sc in next 6-ch sp, ch2, *(1dc, ch2, 1dc) in top of next 5-dc cl, ch2, 1sc in next 6-ch sp, ch2; rep from * to end, join with ss in 3rd of 5-ch.
Fasten off F, join G in any 2-ch sp between 2-dc from prev round.

Round 9: Ch11 (counts as first sc and 10-ch), [skip next (1dc, 2-ch, 1sc, 2-ch, 1dc), 1sc in next 2-ch sp from prev round, ch10] 11 times, join with ss in first of beg 11-ch.
Fasten off G.
Thread 12 beads onto D, join yarn in any 10-ch sp.

Round 10: [Ch8, bring bead to hook, ch1, ss in 2nd ch from bead, ch6, 1sc in next 10-ch sp] 12 times, join with ss in first of beg 8-ch.
Fasten off.

MAKING UP AND FINISHING

Sew in all yarn ends carefully.

Block your work, pinning out each beaded point.

granny love blanket

This blanket is a classic granny square with extra rounds to create the required size, and mini granny squares to form the border. Learning to crochet is the lifetime gift we give ourselves. It takes time and repetition to perfect, and with each stitch you work you are embedding the muscle memory.

SKILL RATING: ● ● ●

MATERIALS:

Stylecraft Life DK (75% acrylic, 25% wool, approx. 326yds/298m per 3½oz/100g ball) light worsted (DK) weight yarn

- 3 balls of Cream shade 2305 (B)
- 1 ball each of:
  - Heather shade 2309 (A)
  - Rose shade 2301 (C)
  - Lily shade 2417 (D)
  - Fuchsia shade 2344 (E)

Stylecraft Life Tweed (75% acrylic, 25% wool, approx. 326yds/298m per 3½oz/100g ball) light worsted (DK) weight yarn

- 1 ball of Denim Nepp 2368 (F)

US size 7 (4.5mm) crochet hook

Yarn needle

FINISHED MEASUREMENTS:

51in (129cm) square

GAUGE (TENSION):

Four 3-dc groups x 7 rows = 4in (10cm) square over patt, using US size 7 (4.5mm) hook.

ABBREVIATIONS:

See page 127.

SPECIAL ABBREVIATION:

esc (elongated single crochet): insert hook in st two rows below current row, yo, pull yarn up level to current row, yo, pull through both loops on hook to complete esc

FOR THE BLANKET

CENTRAL SQUARE

Using A, ch6 and join with ss in first ch to form a ring.

Round 1: Ch3 (counts as first dc throughout), 2dc into ring, *ch3, 3dc into the ring; rep from * twice more, join with ss in 3rd of beg 3-ch.

Fasten off A.

Round 2: Join B in any corner 3-ch sp, ch3, 2dc in same 3-ch sp (half corner made), *ch1, (3dc, ch2, 3dc) in next 3-ch sp (corner made); rep from * twice more, ch1, 3dc in same sp as beg half corner, ch2, join with ss in 3rd of beg 3-ch.

Fasten off B.

Round 3: Join C in any corner 2-ch sp, ch3, 2dc in same 2-ch sp (half corner made), *ch1, 3dc in next 1-ch sp, ch1, (3dc, ch2, 3dc) in next 2-ch sp (corner made); rep from * twice more, ch1, 3dc in next 1-ch sp, ch1, 3dc in same sp as beg half corner, ch2, join with ss in 3rd of beg 3-ch.

Fasten off C.

Round 4: Join D in any corner 2-ch sp, ch3, 2dc in same 2-ch sp (half corner made), *ch1, [3dc in next 1-ch sp, ch1] to next corner 2-ch sp, (3dc, ch2, 3dc) in 2-ch sp (corner made); rep from * twice more, ch1, [3dc in next 1-ch sp, ch1] to beg half corner, 3dc in same sp as beg half corner, ch2, join with ss in 3rd of beg 3-ch.

Fasten off D.

Round 5: Using E, rep round 4.
Round 6: Using B, rep round 4.
Round 7: Using E, rep round 4.
Round 8: Using D, rep round 4.
Round 9: Using C, rep round 4.
Round 10: Using B, rep round 4.
Round 11: Using A, rep round 4.
Round 12: Using B, rep round 4.
Round 13: Using C, rep round 4.
Round 14: Using D, rep round 4.
Rounds 15–34: Rep rounds 5–14 twice.
Round 35: Using E, rep round 4.
Rounds 36–38: Using B, rep round 4.
Fasten off.

MINI SQUARES (make 80)

Using F, ch6 and join with ss in first ch to form a ring.

Round 1: Ch3 (counts as first dc throughout), 2dc into the ring, *ch3, 3dc into the ring; rep from * twice more, join with ss in 3rd of beg 3-ch.

Fasten off F.

Join first mini square to central square using join-as-you-go method (see page 122).

MINDFULNESS

As the rounds get longer and your familiarity with the stitch and pattern deepens, you can begin the mindful journey of linking the stitch with the breath. Practice a three-part breath by breathing deeply into your belly first, then into the ribcage and finally into your upper chest. Slowly exhale, fully reversing the flow. Now practice making the out breath longer than the in breath, and use crocheting stitches as a timer. Connecting breath with movement distracts your mind and allows you to become more present.

- Where the two mini squares are joined together you will have two corner 2-ch spaces side by side. When working the border treat these two spaces as one space by working 1dc into the first space and 2dc into the next space to form the 3-dc group, then ch1 to the next space.
- It can feel as if you are working into a space that is slightly backward when making the 2dc in the 2-ch sp at the base of the beginning 3ch in round 3.

Round 2: Join B in any corner 3-ch sp of mini square, ch3, 2dc in same 3-ch sp, insert hook in any 1-ch sp of central square from underneath, 1sc in 1-ch sp of central square (counts as first of 2-ch for corner sp), ch1, work second 3-dc group in same 3-ch sp of current square. Replace next 1-ch of current mini square with 1sc in next side sp of central square, 3dc in next 3-ch sp of mini square, 1sc in 1-ch sp of central square (counts as first of 2-ch for corner sp), ch1, 3dc in same 3-ch sp, *ch1, (3dc, ch2, 3dc) in next 3-ch sp (corner made); rep from * once more, ch1, join with ss in 3rd of beg 3-ch.

Cont joining squares in this way to both the central square and prev mini squares. When joining next mini square to central square and previous mini square at a shared corner, replace both corner ch of current square with 1sc in each adjoining square.

Join 80 squares to form border around central square.

FINAL BORDER

Round 1: Join B in any corner 2-ch sp, ch3 (counts as first dc throughout), 2dc in same 2-ch sp (half corner made), *work [ch1, 3dc in next 1-ch sp, ch1, work across join between mini squares with 1dc in first 2-ch sp, 2dc in next 2-ch sp] to next corner, ch1, (3dc, ch2, 3dc) in next 2-ch sp (corner made); rep from * twice, work [ch1, 3dc in next 1-ch sp, ch1, work across join between mini squares with 1dc in first 2-ch sp, 2dc in next 2-ch sp] to beg half corner, ch1, 3dc in same sp as beg half corner, ch2, join with ss in 3rd of beg 3-ch.

Round 2: Ch3, 2dc in 2-ch sp at base of 3-ch (half corner made) *ch1, [3dc in next 1-ch sp, ch1] to next corner 2-ch sp, (3dc, ch2, 3dc) in next 2-ch sp (corner made); rep from * twice more, ch1, [3dc in next 1-ch sp, ch1] to beg half corner, 3dc in same sp as beg half corner, ch2, join with ss in 3rd of beg 3-ch.
Fasten off B and rejoin B in any corner 2-ch sp.

Round 3: Ch1 (counts as first sc throughout), 1sc in each st and 1-ch sp around, working (1sc, ch2, 1sc) in each corner, ending 1sc into beg 2-ch sp, ch2, join with ss in beg 1-ch.
Fasten off B.

Round 4: Join F in any corner 2-ch sp, ch1, *[ch1, skip next st, 1esc in next st of round 2] to corner 2-ch sp, (1sc, ch2, 1sc) in corner 2-ch sp; rep from * twice more, [ch1, skip next st, 1esc in next st of round 2] to last corner 2-ch sp, 1sc in 2-ch sp, ch2, join with ss in beg 1-ch.
Fasten off.

MAKING UP AND FINISHING

Sew in all yarn ends carefully.

kaleidoscope mandala mat

Mandalas require your undivided attention because their success lies in correctly counting the stitches for each round. This makes them perfect for focusing the mind and bringing you into the present moment.

SKILL RATING: ● ● ●

MATERIALS:

Rico Essentials Cotton DK (100% cotton, approx. 142yds/130m per 1¾oz/50g ball) light worsted (DK) weight yarn

1 x ball each of:

- Cobalt Blue shade 32 (A)
- Fuchsia shade 14 (B)
- Natural shade 51 (C)
- Light Blue shade 27 (D)
- Banana shade 63 (E)
- Pumpkin shade 87 (F)
- Pistachio shade 86 (G)
- Violet shade 97 (H)

US size F/5 (3.75mm) crochet hook

Yarn needle

FINISHED MEASUREMENTS:

18in (46cm) diameter

GAUGE (TENSION):

Rounds 1–4 = 2¾in (7cm) diameter, using US size F/5 (3.75mm) hook.

ABBREVIATIONS:

See page 127.

SPECIAL ABBREVIATIONS:

3-dc cl (3-double crochet cluster): [yo, insert hook in sp/st, yo, pull a loop through, yo, pull through 2 loops on hook] 3 times in same sp/st (4 loops on hook), yo, pull though all 4 loops to complete cluster

4-dc cl (4-double crochet cluster): [yo, insert hook in ch sp, yo, pull a loop through, yo, pull through first 2 loops on hook] 4 times in same ch sp (5 loops on hook), yo, pull through all 5 loops to complete cluster

FPsc (front post single crochet): from front of work insert hook from right to left behind post of next st on round below and through to front again, yo and pull loop through (2 loops on hook), yo, pull through both loops

MINDFULNESS

Before you begin, switch off the television, put the phone on silent and allow yourself to fully arrive, to be fully present. Sit tall; take three slow deep deliberate breaths and with each exhalation feel yourself fully connected to the chair you are sittting in. Now begin your crochet.

FOR THE MAT

MAIN MANDALA

Using A, make a magic ring, or ch6 and join with ss in first ch to form a ring.

Round 1: Ch3 (counts as first dc), 11dc into the ring, join with ss in 3rd of beg 3-ch. *12 sts.*

Fasten off A.

Round 2: Join B in any st, ch3 (counts as first dc), 1dc in same st, 2dc in each st to end, join with ss in 3rd of beg 3-ch. *24 sts.*

Fasten off B.

Round 3: Join C in any st, ch2 (counts as first sc + ch1), *1sc in next st, ch1; rep from * to end, join with ss in beg 1-ch. *24 sc + twenty-four 1-ch sps.*

Fasten off C.

Round 4: Join D in any 1-ch sp, ch2 (counts as first sc + ch1), *1sc in next 1-ch sp, ch1; rep from * to end, join with ss in first of beg 2-ch.

Fasten off D.

Round 5: Join E in any 1-ch sp, ch3 (counts as first dc), 1dc in same sp, 2dc in each 1-ch sp to end, join with ss in 3rd of beg 3-ch. *48 sts.*

Fasten off E.

Round 6: Join B in any st, ch1 (counts as first sc throughout), 1sc in each st to end, join with ss in beg 1-ch.

Fasten off B.

Round 7: Join A in any st, ch3 (counts as first sc + ch2), skip next st, *1sc in next st, ch2, skip next st; rep from * to end, join with ss in first of beg 3-ch. *24 sc + twenty-four 2-ch sps.*

Fasten off A.

Round 8: Join F in any 2-ch sp, ch3 (counts as first dc), 2dc in same sp, 3dc in each 2-ch sp to end, join with ss into 3rd of beg 3-ch. *72 sts.*

Fasten off F.

Round 9: Join C in sp between any 3-dc groups, ch2 (counts as first sc + ch1), skip next st, 1sc in next st, ch1, skip next st, *1sc in next sp between 3-dc groups, ch1, skip next st, 1sc in next st, ch1, skip next st; rep from * to end, join with ss in first of beg 2-ch. *48 sc + forty-eight 1-ch sps.*

Fasten off C.

Round 10: Join G in any 1-ch sp, ch2 (counts as first hdc), 1hdc in same sp, 2hdc in each 1-ch sp to end, join with ss in 2nd of beg 2-ch.

Fasten off G.

Round 11: Join B in sp between any 2-hdc groups, ch3 (counts as first dc of 3-dc cl), complete the 3-dc cl in same sp, ch2, skip next 2 sts, *3-dc cl in next sp between 2-hdc groups, ch2, skip next 2 sts; rep from * to end, join with ss in 3rd of beg 3-ch. *Forty-eight 3-dc cl.*

Fasten off B.

Round 12: Join C in any 2-ch sp, ch1, 1sc in same 2-ch sp, 1FPsc around top of 3-dc cl, *2sc in next 2-ch sp, 1FPsc around top of next 3-dc cl; rep from * to end, join with ss in beg 1-ch. *144 sts.*

Fasten off C.

Round 13: Join D in any sc st, ch2 (counts as first sc + ch1), skip next st, *1sc in next st, ch1, skip next st; rep from * to end, join with ss in first of beg 2-ch. *72 sc + seventy-two 1-ch sps.*

Fasten off D.

Round 14: Join F in any 1-ch sp, ch1, 1sc in same sp, 2sc in each 1-ch sp to end, join with ss in beg 1-ch. *144 sts.*

Fasten off F.

Round 15: Working with B and G, join B in any st, ch2 (counts as first hdc), 1hdc in each of next 10 sts, change to G, 4-dc cl in next st, change to B (carrying G behind work and working over it), *1hdc in each of next 11 sts, change to G, 4-dc cl in next st, change to B; rep from * to end, using B, join with ss in 2nd of beg 2-ch. *132 hdc + twelve 4-dc cl.*

Fasten off B and G.

Round 16: Join F in any st, ch1, 1sc in each st to end, join with ss in beg 1-ch. *144 sts.*

Fasten off F.

Round 17: Using D, rep round 13.

Round 18: Using C, rep round 14.

Round 19: Using A, rep round 7.

Round 20: Join C in any 2-ch sp directly above 4-dc cl in round 15, ch4 (counts as first tr), 2dc in same sp, 2hdc in next 2-ch sp, 2sc in each of next two 2-ch sps, 2hdc in next 2-ch sp, (2dc, 1tr) in next 2-ch sp, ch2, *(1tr, 2dc) in next 2-ch sp, 2hdc in next 2-ch sp, 2sc in each of next two 2-ch sps, 2hdc in next 2-ch sp, (2dc, 1tr) in next 2-ch sp, ch2; rep from * to end, join with ss in 4th of beg 4-ch. *168 sts + twelve 2-ch sps.*

Fasten off C.

Round 21: Join G in any 2-ch sp, ch1, (1sc, ch2, 2sc) in same sp, 1sc in each of next 14 sts, *(2sc ch2, 2sc) in next 2-ch sp, 1sc in each of next 14 sts; rep from * to end, join with ss in beg 1-ch.

Fasten off.

MINI MANDALAS (make 12—2 of each color combination as in chart)

Using first yarn for round 1 as indicated by chart, make a magic ring, or ch6 and join with ss in first ch to form a ring.

Round 1: Ch3 (counts as first dc throughout), 11dc into ring, join with ss in 3rd of beg 3-ch. *12 sts.*

Fasten off first color.

Round 2: Join second color in any st, ch3, 1dc in same st, 2dc in each st to end, join with ss in 3rd of beg 3-ch. *24 sts.*

Fasten off second color.

Round 3: Join third color in any st, ch2 (counts as first sc + ch1), *1sc in next st, ch1; rep from * to end, join with ss in beg 1-ch. *24 sc + twenty-four 1-ch sps.*

Fasten off third color.

Round 4: Join fourth color in any 1-ch sp, ch2 (counts as first sc + ch1), *1sc in next 1-ch sp, ch1; rep from * to end, join with ss in beg 1-ch.

Fasten off fourth color.

Round 5: Join fifth color in any 1-ch sp, ch2 (counts as first hdc), 1hdc in same sp, 2hdc in each 1-ch sp to end, join with ss in 2nd of beg 2-ch.

Fasten off.

MAKING UP AND FINISHING

Sew in all yarn ends carefully.

Twist strands of two different colored yarns together and weave through rounds 2, 5, and 8 of the mat.
Twist strands of two different colored yarns together and weave through round 2 of each mini mandala.

JOIN MINI MANDALAS TO CENTRAL MANDALA

With RS tog, place the mini mandalas alongside round 21 of the central mandala. Using G, sew together the 2 outer stitches from each mandala, starting and finishing at the 2-ch sps on round 21.

BORDER

On one mini mandala, count 6 sts up from the join at the base of the 2-ch sp from round 21.

Round 1: Join G into 6th st, ch1 (counts as first sc), 1sc in same st, *ch3, skip 3 sts, 2sc in next st; rep from * 4 times, ch1 **join to next mini mandala by working 2sc in 6th st up from join at 2-ch sp on round 21; rep from * around each mini mandala, ending last rep at **, join with ss in beg 1-ch.

Fasten off G.

Round 2: Join C in first 3-ch sp on farthest right of any mini mandala, *ch3 (counts as first dc), 5dc in same sp, [ss between next 2sc, 6dc in next 3-ch sp] 4 times, ss between last 2 sc on current mini mandala, **1sc in 1-ch sp between two mini mandalas, ss between first 2 sc of next mini mandala; rep from * to end, ending last rep at **, join with ss in 3rd of 3-ch. Fasten off.

Sew in all remaining yarn ends and block.

ROUND	Mandala 1	Mandala 2	Mandala 3	Mandala 4	Mandala 5	Mandala 6
Round 1	B	H	E	B	F	D
Round 2	G	E	F	E	H	B
Round 3	C	C	C	C	C	C
Round 4	A	D	A	H	A	G
Round 5	F	B	H	F	B	H

secret garden fall shawl

The wonderful rainbow effect of this shawl is very cheering on a dull day. There is great value to be had when working a repetitive pattern on a large project. Once the brain and hands become synchronized and a familiarity with the pattern is embedded, the mindful space is created.

SKILL RATING: ● ● ●

MATERIALS:

Scheepjes Secret Garden (60% polyester, 20% silk, approx. 101yds/93m per 1¾oz/50g ball) light worsted (DK) weight yarn

- 2 balls each of:
  - Rambling Blooms shade 705 (A)
  - Summer House shade 707 (B)
  - Secluded Lake shade 703 (C)
- 1 ball of Shady Courtyard shade 737 (D)

US size 7 (4.5mm) crochet hook

Yarn needle

FINISHED MEASUREMENTS:

64in (160cm) wide x 30in (75cm) deep

GAUGE (TENSION):

14 sts x 6 rows = 4in (10cm) over double crochet, using US size 7 (4.5mm) hook.

ABBREVIATIONS:

See page 127.

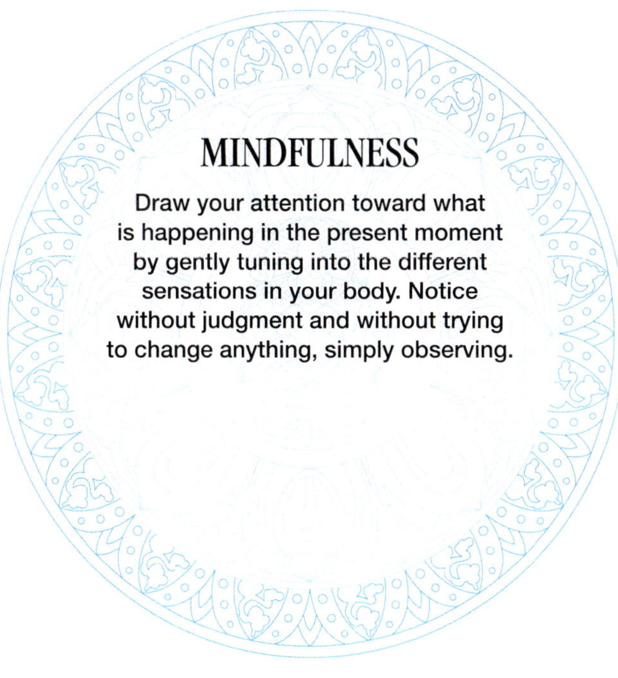

MINDFULNESS

Draw your attention toward what is happening in the present moment by gently tuning into the different sensations in your body. Notice without judgment and without trying to change anything, simply observing.

FOR THE SHAWL

Using A, make a magic ring, or ch6 and join with ss in first ch to form a ring.

Row 1: Ch3 (counts as first dc throughout), 5dc into the ring, ch2, 6dc into ring, ch2, turn. *12 sts + one 2-ch sp.*

Row 2: Ch3, 2dc in same st, 1dc in each of next 5 sts to corner 2-ch sp, (2dc, ch2, 2dc) in corner 2-ch sp, 1dc in each of next 5 sts, 3dc in top of beg 3-ch of prev row, turn. *20 sts + one 2-ch sp.*

Row 3: Ch3, 2dc in same st, 1dc in each of next 9 sts to corner 2-ch sp, (2dc, ch2, 2dc) in corner 2-ch sp, 1dc in each of next 9 sts, 3dc in top of beg 3-ch of prev row, turn. *28 sts + one 2-ch sp.*

Row 4: Ch3, 1dc in same st, ch1, 1dc in next st, *ch1, skip next st, 1dc in next st; rep from * to corner 2-ch sp (ending with 1dc in last st before corner 2-ch sp), ch1, (1dc, ch2, 1dc) in corner 2-ch sp, ch1, 1dc in next st, **ch1, skip next st, 1dc in next st; rep from ** to last st, ch1, 2dc in top of beg 3-ch of prev row, turn.

Row 5: Ch3, 2dc in same st, 1dc in next st, *1dc in next 1-ch sp, 1dc in next st; rep from * to corner 2-ch sp, (2dc, 2-ch, 2dc) in corner 2-ch sp, 1dc in next st, **1dc in next 1-ch sp, 1dc in next st; rep from ** to last st, 3dc in top of beg 3-ch of prev row, turn.

Row 6: Rep row 4.

Row 7: Rep row 5.

Row 8: Ch3, 2dc in same st, 1dc in each st to corner 2-ch sp, (2dc, ch2, 2dc) in corner 2-ch sp, 1dc in each st to last st, 3dc in top of beg 3-ch of prev row.

Row 9: Rep row 4.

Row 10: Rep row 5.

Rows 11 and 12: Rep row 8.

Row 13: Using B, rep row 4.

Row 14: Using A, rep row 5.

Row 15: Using B, rep row 4.

Row 16: Using A, rep row 5.

Row 17: Using A, rep row 8.

Row 18: Using B, rep row 4.

Row 19: Using A, rep row 5.

Row 20: Using A, rep row 8.

Row 21: Using B, rep row 8.

Row 22: Rep row 4.

Row 23: Rep row 5.

Row 24: Rep row 4.

Row 25: Using C, rep row 5.

Row 26: Using B, rep row 4.

Row 27: Using C, rep row 5.

Row 28: Rep row 4.

Row 29: Rep row 5.

Row 30: Rep row 4.

Row 31: Rep row 5.

Row 32: Rep row 4.

Row 33: Rep row 5.

Row 34: Using D, rep row 4.

Row 35: Rep row 5.

Row 36: Rep row 4.

Fasten off.

MAKING UP AND FINISHING

Sew in all yarn ends carefully and block to shape.

- Working the 3dc into the top of the beginning 3-ch of the previous row can be quite fiddly, so you can work these last 3 stitches into the space between the posts rather than into the stitch.
- Always count the 1-ch sps on both sides in row 4 to make sure they are equal and that you haven't skipped one somewhere as it is very easy to slip up on this row!

basketweave lap blanket

The lovely basketweave effect on this blanket is simply created by working three front post double crochets followed by three back post double crochets, and it's finished with fun pompoms at the corners. We are all different; it doesn't matter how you hold your hook or yarn, or if you don't know your worsted (Aran) weight from your light worsted (DK). All that matters is your love of crochet, the yarn and your desire to keep going.

SKILL RATING: ● ● ●

MATERIALS:

James Brett Marble Chunky (100% acrylic, approx. 341yds/312m per 7oz/200g ball) bulky (chunky) weight yarn

2 balls each of:
- MC8 (A)
- MC44 (A)

Stylecraft Special DK (100% acrylic, approx. 322yds/295m per 3½oz/100g ball) light worsted (DK) weight yarn

1 ball each of:
- Empire shade 1829 (B)
- Turquoise shade 1068 (B)
- Aspen shade 1422 (B)
- Bluebell shade 1082 (B)
- Teal shade 1062 (B)
- Wisteria shade 1432 (B)
- Violet shade 1277 (B)

US size M/13 (9mm) crochet hook

Yarn needle

2¼in (5.5cm) pompom maker

FINISHED MEASUREMENTS:

39in (100cm) wide x 45in (115cm) long

GAUGE (TENSION):

8 dc x 3 rows = 4in (10cm) over patt, using US size M/13 (9mm) hook.

ABBREVIATIONS:

See page 127.

SPECIAL ABBREVIATION:

BPdc (back post double crochet): yo, from back of work insert hook from right to left in front of post of next st on prev round and through to back again, yo and pull a loop through, [yoh, pull through 2 loops] twice

FPdc (front post double crochet): yo, from front of work insert hook from right to left behind post of next st on prev round and through to front again, yo and pull loop through, [yo, pull through 2 loops] twice

FOR THE BLANKET

Using one strand of any A shade and one strand of any B shade held tog, ch71.

Row 1: 1dc in 4th ch from hook (skipped 3-ch counts as first dc), 1dc in each st to end, turn. *69 dc.*

Row 2: Ch3 (counts as first dc throughout), skip st at base of 3-ch, 1FPdc in each of next 2 sts, *1BPdc in each of next 3 sts, 1FPdc in each of next 3 sts; rep from * to end, turn.

Row 3: Ch3, skip st at base of 3-ch, 1BPdc in each of next 2 sts, *1FPdc in each of next 3 sts, 1BPdc in each of next 3 sts; rep from * to end, turn.

Row 4: Ch3, skip st at base of 3-ch, 1BPdc in each of next 2 sts, *1FPdc in each of next 3 sts, 1BPdc in each of next 3 sts; rep from * to end, turn.

Row 5: Ch3 (counts as first dc throughout), skip st at base of 3-ch, 1FPdc in each of next 2 sts, *1BPdc in each of next 3 sts, 1FPdc in each of next 3 sts; rep from * to end, turn.

Rows 6–69: Rep rows 2–5.

Fasten off.

MAKING UP AND FINISHING

Sew in all yarn ends carefully.

POMPOMS

Using a mix of B yarns, make four 2¼in (5.5cm) pompoms. Sew a pompom to each corner of the blanket.

- **Work with two strands held together throughout, one Marble Chunky color and one Special DK color.**
- **Change one yarn color at a time, aiming for a color change every row.**

MINDFULNESS

Learn from others but do not be put off—you are your own teacher. Follow your heart with this blanket: trust the color blends you choose and as you crochet allow yourself to fully relax into the rhythmical flow of working into the posts. This is a physical activity where the mind and body can harmonize.

chapter 4

caring and sharing

retro flower garland

A single flower makes a lovely gift presented on a card, or they can be strung together as a summer flower garland. Each is simple to make and they are great for the confident beginner to take the next step with their crochet. Work slowly until you are familiar with this yarn as it can sometimes split a little.

SKILL RATING: ● ● ●

MATERIALS:

Scheepjes Cahlista (100% cotton, approx. 92yds/85m per 1¾oz/50g ball) worsted (Aran) weight yarn

⅓ ball each of:

- Lime Juice shade 392
- Shocking Pink shade 114
- Lavender shade 520
- Bridal White shade 105
- Yellow Gold shade 208

US size G/6 (4mm) crochet hook

Yarn needle

FINISHED MEASUREMENTS:

52in (132cm) long

GAUGE (TENSION):

Sunflower = 3in (7.5cm) diameter, using US size G/6 (4mm) hook.

ABBREVIATIONS:

See page 127.

SPECIAL ABBREVIATION:

esc (elongated single crochet): insert hook in st two rows below current row, yo, pull yarn up level to current row, yo, pull through both loops on hook to complete esc

FOR THE GARLAND

Use any color in any combination.

SMALL 5-PETAL BLOSSOM (make 8)

Using first color, make a magic ring, or ch6 and join with ss in first ch to form a ring.

Round 1: Ch1 (does not count as st throughout), 10sc into the ring. *10 sts.*

Fasten off.

Round 2: Join second color in any st, *(1hdc, 1dc, 1hdc) in next st, ss in next st; rep from * 4 times. *5 petals.*

Fasten off.

SUNFLOWER (make 3)

Using first color, make a magic ring, or ch6 and join with ss in first ch to form a ring.

Round 1: Ch1 (does not count as st throughout), 10sc into the ring, join with ss in beg 1-ch. *10 sts.*

Round 2: Ch1, 2sc in each st to end, join with ss in first sc. *20 sts.*

Round 3: Ch1, [1sc in next st, 2sc in next st] 10 times, join with ss in first sc. *30 sts.*

Fasten off.

Round 4: Join second color in any st, *1sc in next st, (1hdc, 1dc) in next st, (1dc, 1hdc) in next st, 1sc in next st, ss in next st; rep from * 5 times. *6 petals.*

Fasten off.

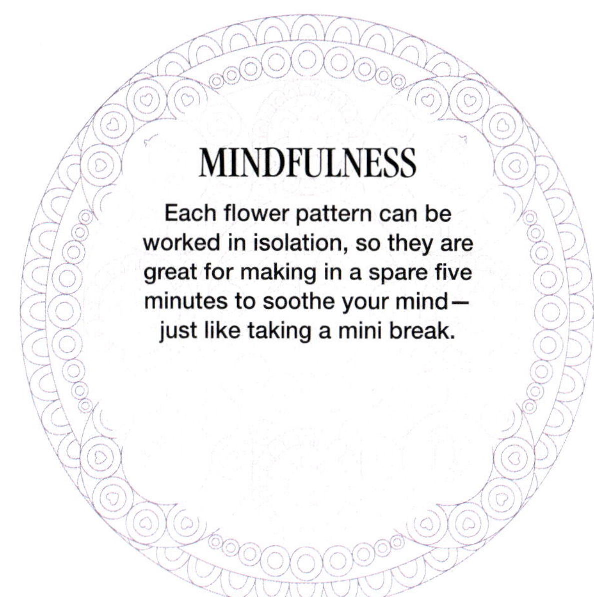

LARGE 7-PETAL FLOWER (make 4)

Using first color, make a magic ring, or ch6 and join with ss in first ch to form a ring.

Round 1: Ch1 (does not count as st throughout), 7sc into the ring. *7 sts.*

Round 2: Ch1, 2sc in each st to end, join with ss in first sc. *14 sts.*

Fasten off.

Round 3: Join second color in any st, ch1, [1sc in next st, 2sc in next st] 7 times, join with ss in first sc. *21 sts.*

Fasten off.

Round 4: Join third color in second sc of any 2-sc inc in round 2, pull yarn up to level of current round, ch1 (counts as 1sc), *ch5, skip next 2 sts, 1esc in second sc of next 2-sc inc in round 2 (ensuring you bring yarn up to level of current round); rep from * 5 times, ch5, skip last 2 sts, join with ss in beg 1-ch. *7 petals.*

Round 5: *5sc in next 5-ch sp, ss in top loop of esc from round 4; rep from * to end, join with ss in last esc.

Fasten off.

MAKING UP AND FINISHING

To add embellishments to the sunflower, with RS facing and using any contrasting color, work a round of surface crochet (see page 126) around the outer edge of round 3. Cut the yarn and thread it through the last stitch to fasten off, then thread the end onto a yarn needle. Insert the needle into the first stitch—the same place as if you were crocheting this stitch—and pull through. Then insert the needle into the back loop of the previous stitch and pull through to make an invisible join in the circle of surface crochet. To finish, sew in the end.

With RS facing and using any contrasting color in a yarn needle, make 5 French knots (see page 123) between the stitches in round 1 and 10 French knots in the stitches between rounds 2 and 3.

To assemble the garland, using pale green, ch15, join with a ss in 15th ch from hook to form hanging loop, *ch10, join a small petal blossom by working 1sc in any st, ch10, join a large 7-petal flower by working 1sc in each of the top two sts of any petal, ch10, join a small petal blossom by working 1sc in any st, ch10, join sunflower by working 1sc in each of the 2 dc sts of any petal; rep from * until all flowers are joined ending with a small petal blossom, ch25, join with a ss in 15th ch from hook to form hanging loop. With WS facing and working back down ch, ch1, 1sc in each ch to first hanging loop.

Fasten off.

Sew in all yarn ends carefully.

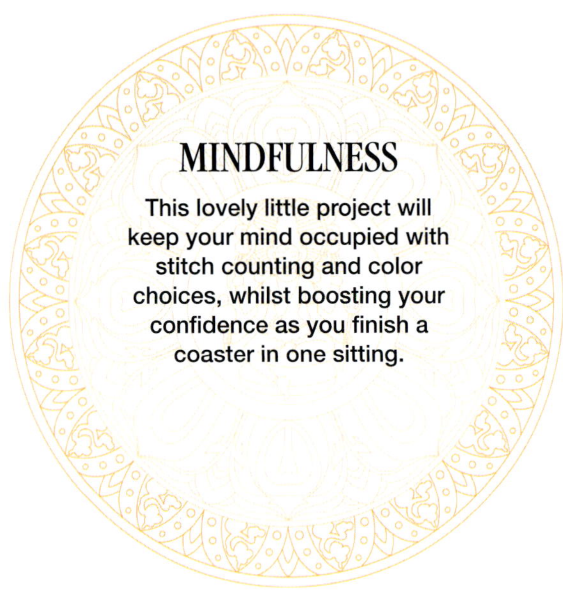

MINDFULNESS

This lovely little project will keep your mind occupied with stitch counting and color choices, whilst boosting your confidence as you finish a coaster in one sitting.

summer sun coasters

Simple and quick to make, each coaster is designed to make the colors sing no matter which combination you choose. Repeat the pattern using a different color for each round and notice which combination makes you happiest! If you've mastered the double crochet stitch and can make a simple circle, then this project is the perfect next step.

SKILL RATING: ● ● ●

MATERIALS:

Scheepjes Cahlista (100% cotton, approx. 92yds/85m per 1¾oz/50g ball) worsted (Aran) weight yarn

- 1 ball each of:
  - Sweet Orange shade 411
  - Shocking Pink shade 114
  - Crystalline shade 385
  - Light Orchid shade 226
  - Old Lace shade 130

US size 7 (4.5mm) crochet hook

Yarn needle

FINISHED MEASUREMENTS:

4½in (11.5cm) diameter

GAUGE (TENSION):

Exact gauge (tension) is not important on this project.

ABBREVIATIONS:

See page 127.

SPECIAL ABBREVIATION:

esc (elongated single crochet): insert hook in st two rows below current row, yo, pull yarn up level to current row, yo, pull through both loops on hook to complete esc

FOR THE COASTERS

Use any sequence of colors.

Using first color, make a magic ring, or ch6 and join with ss in first ch to form a ring.

Round 1: Ch2 (counts as first hdc throughout), 11hdc into the ring, join with ss in 2nd of beg 2-ch. *12 sts.*

Fasten off.

Round 2: Join second color in any st, ch2, 1hdc in same sp, 2hdc in next and each st to end, join with ss in 2nd of beg 2-ch. *24 sts.*

Fasten off.

Round 3: Join third color in any sp between 2 hdc in prev round, ch2, 2hdc in same sp, *skip next 2 hdc, 3hdc in next sp between 2 hdc in prev round; rep from * to end, join with ss in 2nd of beg 2-ch. *36 sts.*

Fasten off.

• Work slowly through the stitches as worsted (Aran) weight cotton can split a little if you rush it.

• After round 4 your work may feel a little floppy around the edges, but the next two rounds will tighten it all up and bring it together to lie flat.

Round 4: Join fourth color in second hdc of any 2-hdc group in round 2, pull yarn level to new round, ch1 (counts as first esc), *skip first hdc of 3-hdc group in prev round, 1sc in each of next 2 sts, 1esc in second hdc of next 2-hdc group in round 2; rep from * to end, finishing last rep with 1sc in each of last 2 sts, join with ss in beg 1-ch.*12 esc + 24 sc.*
Fasten off.
Round 5: Join fifth color in any st in prev round, ch1 (counts as first sc), 1sc in each st to end, join with ss in beg 1-ch.
Fasten off.
Round 6: Join first color in any st above esc in round 4, ch2 (counts as first hdc), (1hdc, ch2, 2hdc) in same st, *skip 2 sts, (2hdc, ch2, 2hdc) in next st; rep from * to end, join with ss in 2nd of beg 2-ch. *48 hdc + twelve 2-ch sps.*
Fasten off.

MAKING UP AND FINISHING

Sew in all yarn ends carefully.

tea light holder cover

Working with a small hook and a fine yarn requires little strength but expert dexterity and a focused mind. Take it slow to begin with, as working into the foundation chain is the trickiest bit. Perfect this and the rest becomes easy! Once complete the candlelight will flicker through the open stitches like sunlight through stained glass. This pattern can easily be adjusted for any size candle holder.

SKILL RATING: ● ● ●

MATERIALS:

Hedgehog Fibres Sock Yarn (90% merino wool, 10% nylon, approx. 437yds/400m per 3½oz/100g hank) fingering (4 ply) weight yarn
Small amount each of:
Villain (A)
Heyday (B)

US size B/1–C/2 (2.5mm) crochet hook

Yarn needle

FINISHED MEASUREMENTS:

Cover: 2¼in (5.5cm) high, 7½in (19cm) circumference, to fit a tea light holder 2½in (6.5cm) diameter

GAUGE (TENSION):

Exact gauge (tension) is not important on this project—the foundation chain should be an even number of chain and fit snugly around the base.

ABBREVIATIONS:

See page 127.

SPECIAL ABBREVIATION:

PC (4-dc popcorn): work 4dc all in same st, remove hook from loop and insert in top of first dc made, pick up dropped loop again, yo and join with a ss, pull tight so popcorn pops forward

- The container can be an old jam jar or tea light holder, but the sides must be straight and not taper too much.
- Keep fitting your work over your tea light holder to ensure a snug fit. If it's too loose, reduce the number of foundation chain.
- The best yarn is a fingering or 4 ply weight, as we want the candlelight to shine through.
- Stay fire-safe by ensuring that your crochet does not go over the top of your candle holder.

FOR THE COVER

Using A, ch40, making sure ch is not twisted, join with ss in first ch.
Round 1: Ch1, 1sc in each ch to end, ss in first ch to join. *40 sts.*
Round 2: Ch3 (counts as first dc), 1dc in each st to end, join with ss in 3rd of beg 3-ch.
Round 3: Rep round 2.
Round 4: Ch4 (counts as 1dc and ch1 throughout), *skip next st, 1dc, ch1; rep from * to end, join with ss in 3rd of beg 4-ch. *20 dc + twenty 1-ch sps.*
Round 5: Rep round 4.
Fasten off A.
Round 6: Join B with ss in any 1-ch sp, ch3 (counts as first dc of PC), complete PC in same sp, *ch3, skip next 1-ch sp, PC in next 1-ch sp; rep from * to last 1-ch sp, ch3, skip last 1-ch sp, join with ss in 3rd of beg 3-ch. *10 PC + ten 3-ch sps.*
Fasten off B.
Round 7: Join A in top of any PC, ch4, [1dc in next 3-ch sp, ch1, 1dc in top of next PC, ch1] 9 times 1dc in last 3-ch sp, ch1, join with ss in 3rd of beg 4-ch. *20 dc + twenty 1-ch sps.*
Round 8: Ch4, skip next st, [1dc, ch1, skip next st] 19 times. *20 dc + twenty 1-ch sps.*
Fasten off A.
For taller candle holder, rep rows 6–8 to desired height.
Round 9: Join B in any 1-ch sp, ch1 (counts as first sc), (1hdc, 1dc) in same sp, (1dc, 1hdc, 1sc) in next 1-ch sp, *(1sc, 1hdc, 1dc) in next 1-ch sp, (1dc, 1hdc, 1sc) in next 1-ch sp; rep from * 8 times, join with ss in beg 1-ch. *10 scallops.*
Fasten off.

MAKING UP AND FINISHING

Sew in all yarn ends carefully.

heart garland

Take a few minutes out of your hectic day to make a little heart to give as a gift, or string several together to make a pretty garland for your window or shelf. Each heart takes 10 minutes, so gives you the satisfaction of completing a make in one sitting—perfect if you are sat in a waiting room or at a bus stop. You will need to be confident with double crochet and working in the round.

SKILL RATING: ● ● ●

MATERIALS:

Scheepjes Catona (100% cotton, approx. 27yds/25m per ⅜oz/10g ball) fingering (4 ply) weight yarn
- 1 ball each of:
  - Icy Pink shade 246
  - Lilac Mist shade 399
  - Fresia shade 519
  - Crystalline shade 385

US size E/4 (3.5mm) crochet hook

Yarn needle

FINISHED MEASUREMENTS:

39in (99cm) long

GAUGE (TENSION):

One heart = 2¼in (7cm) wide, using US size E/4 (3.5mm) hook.

ABBREVIATIONS:

See page 127.

SPECIAL ABBREVIATION:

MP (make picot): ch2, join with ss in front 2 loops of dc at base of 2-ch

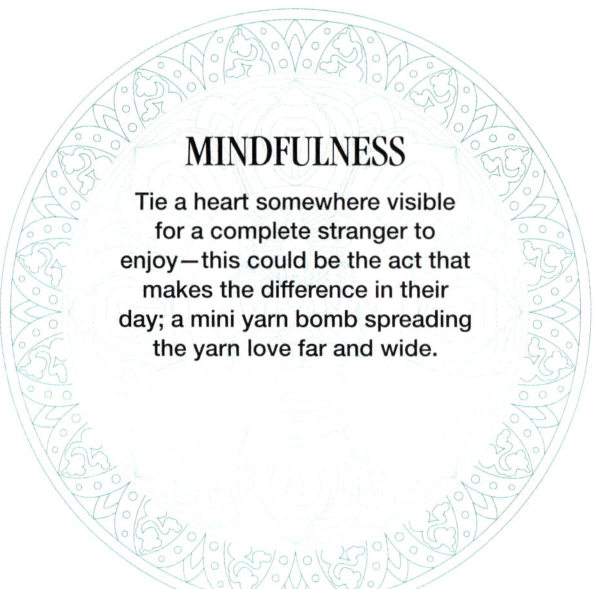

MINDFULNESS

Tie a heart somewhere visible for a complete stranger to enjoy—this could be the act that makes the difference in their day; a mini yarn bomb spreading the yarn love far and wide.

FOR THE GARLAND

HEARTS (make 8)

Using first color, make a magic ring, or ch6 and join with ss in first ch to form a ring.

Round 1: Ch1 (does not count as st throughout), 10hdc into the ring, join with ss in first hdc. *10 sts.*

Round 2: Ch3, skip st at base of 3-ch, (1dc, 2tr) in next st, 2dc in next st, 1hdc in next st, 2sc in next st, (2dc, MP, 1dc) in next st, 2sc in next st, 1hdc in next st, 2dc in next st, (2tr, 1dc) in next st, ch3, join with ss in same st.
Fasten off.

Round 3: Join second color in picot, ch2, 1sc in each of next 6 sts, 2sc in each of next 3 sts, 3sc in 3-ch sp, ss in middle st between two 3-ch, 3sc in next 3-ch sp, 2sc in each of next 3 sts, 1sc in each of next 6 sts, (1sc, 1hdc) in picot, join with ss in beg 2-ch.
Fasten off.

MAKING UP AND FINISHING

Using any color, ch15, join with ss in 15th ch from hook to form hanging loop, ch10, *with heart RS facing work 1sc in each sc of top 2-sc inc of first heart "peak," ch6, skip 6 sts on heart, 1sc in each sc of top 2-sc inc of 2nd heart "peak," ch6; rep from * until all hearts are joined, finishing with 25ch, join with ss in 15th ch from hook to form hanging loop, turn.

With WS facing and working back down ch, ch1, 1sc in each ch to join of first hanging loop. Fasten off.

Sew in all yarn ends carefully.

stress ball key ring charm

Squeeze away the stress with these pocket size mini stress balls. Put them on your key ring as here, or tie them to your bag, and you'll have your stress ball with you wherever you are! Anything goes when choosing the color combinations of your little crochet circles—so have fun and be playful. The pattern is for four stress balls.

SKILL RATING: ● ● ●

MATERIALS:

Rico Ricorumi DK (100% cotton, approx. 63yds/58m per ⅞oz/25g ball) light worsted (DK) weight yarn

1 ball each of:

- White shade 001
- Raspberry shade 013
- Orange shade 027
- Lilac shade 017
- Purple shade 020
- Yellow shade 006
- Tangerine shade 026
- Blue shade 032
- Sky Blue shade 031
- Grass Green shade 044
- Light Green shade 046
- Emerald shade 042

US size F/5 (3.75mm) crochet hook

Polyester toy filling

Yarn needle

Key ring or bag charm fixing

4in (10cm) wide piece of cardstock

Assorted beads

FINISHED MEASUREMENTS:

3in (7.5cm) diameter, not including tassel

GAUGE (TENSION):

Exact gauge (tension) is not important on this project.

ABBREVIATIONS:

See page 127.

SPECIAL ABBREVIATION:

esc (elongated single crochet): insert hook in st two rounds below current round, yo, pull yarn up level to current round, yo, pull through both loops on hook to complete esc

FOR THE BAUBLE

CIRCLES (make 8 in assorted colors)

Using first color, ch6, join with ss in first ch to form a ring.
Round 1: Ch3 (counts as first dc), 11dc into the ring, join with ss into 3rd of beg 3-ch. *12 sts.*
Fasten off first color.
Round 2: Join second color in any st, ch2 (counts as hdc), 1hdc in same st, 2hdc in each st to end, join with ss in 2nd of beg 2-ch. *24 sts.*
Fasten off second color.
Round 3: Join third color in any st from round 1 and pull yarn up level to current round, ch1 (counts as first esc), 1sc in next st, *1esc in next st, 1sc in next st; rep from * to end, join with ss in beg 1-ch.
Fasten off third color.
Round 4: Join fourth color in any st, ch1 (counts as first sc), 1sc in same st (inc), 1sc in each of next 2 sts, *2sc in next st, 1 sc in each of next 2 sts; rep from * to end, join with ss in beg 1-ch.
Fasten off fourth color.

MAKING UP AND FINISHING

Using any color, work surface crochet (see page 126) around rounds 1 and 3 of each circle.
Fasten off and sew in yarn ends.

JOIN THE CIRCLES

Hold two circles with WS tog, matching the corresponding edge stitches. Using any color, work a single crochet seam (see page 124) to join, working 2sc in every fourth st. Stuff with polyester toy filling when about three-quarters of the way around, then complete the seam and join with a ss in the 1-ch.
Fasten off, leaving a 10in (25cm) end.
Rep to make up the other three stress balls.

ADD THE KEY RING/BAG CHARM FITTING

Using the 10in (25cm) end, ch2, remove the hook from the loop and push the loop through the key ring eyelet, replace the loop on the hook, ch2, join with a ss in the base of the ch.
Fasten off.

Sew in all yarn ends carefully.

ADD A TASSEL OR POMPOM

Using any combination of yarn colors, wrap yarn thickly around a 4in (10cm) piece of cardstock. Cut a 10in (25cm) length of yarn, slide it under the strands and tie in a knot at the top. Remove the tassel from the card, and bind it securely just below the top, using a contrasting color of yarn. Thread some beads onto the ends at the top, then use the remaining yarn end to sew the tassel onto the stress ball.

Alternatively make a small pompom (see page 125) using any combination of yarn colors. Leave an 8in (20cm) end at the top, thread on some beads then use to sew the pompom onto the stress ball directly opposite and central to the key ring fixing.

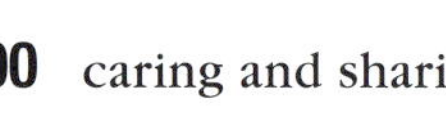

MINDFULNESS

When we express gratitude for the blessings in our lives, when our mind turns toward these things, our hearts open up. It's a beautiful thing to give a handmade piece of crochet to someone as a gift. The very act of making and giving expands our lives and touches the life of the recipient, too.

flowers in a bobbin

Say it with flowers! No matter what is happening in your life, there is always something or someone to be grateful for. Express your love and gratitude to someone special and observe your life expanding. As you crochet really think about the person who will be receiving the flower you are making, and infuse every stitch with the gratitude you have for their contribution to your life. The touch and feel of these delicate yarns is a sensory pleasure and if, like me, you need to rest your mind from chronic pain then making these flowers may just take the edge off.

SKILL RATING: ● ● ●

MATERIALS:

Scheepjes Alpaca Rhythm (80% alpaca, 20% wool, approx. 218yds/200m per 7⁄8oz/25g ball) lace weight yarn
- 1 ball of Bop shade 670 (A)

Scheepjes Mohair Rhythm (70% mohair, 30% microfiber, approx. 218yds/200m per 7⁄8oz/25g ball) lace weight yarn
- 1 ball of Bop shade 690 (A)

Hedgehog Fibres Sock Yarn (90% merino wool, 10% nylon, approx. 437yds/400m per 3½oz/100g hank) fingering (4 ply) weight yarn
- 1 ball each of:
  - Banana Legs (B)
  - Birthday Cake (B)
  - Villain (B)

Scheepjes Catona (100% cotton, approx. 27yds/25m per 3⁄8oz/10g ball) fingering (4 ply) weight yarn
- 1 ball of Apple Granny shade 513 (C)

US size C/2–D/3 (3mm) and US size B/1–C/2 (2.5mm) crochet hooks

Yarn needle

Florist or garden wire

Large wooden bobbin for display

FINISHED MEASUREMENTS:

Flower: approx. 2½in (6.5cm) diameter

GAUGE (TENSION):

Exact gauge (tension) is not important on this project.

ABBREVIATIONS:

See page 127.

MINDFULNESS

Take time to savor the sensation of the soft alpaca and mohair centers... there's really no rush. You may wish to make lots of flowers first and spend time another day making up the stems. This is the beauty of mindful crochet—do what you can when you can, with no pressures or expectations.

FOR THE FLOWER

FLOWER HEAD

With both A strands held tog and using a US size C/2–D/3 (3mm) hook, make a magic ring, or ch6 and join with ss in first ch to form a ring.

Round 1 (RS): Ch2 (counts as first hdc), 11hdc into the ring, join with ss in beg 2-ch. *12 sts*.

Round 2: Ch1 (counts as first sc), [ch2, skip next st, 1sc in next st] 5 times, ch2, skip last st, join with ss in beg 1-ch.

Fasten off.

Round 3 (petals): Using US size B/1–C/2 (2.5mm) hook, join any B yarn with ss in any 2-ch sp, [(ch5, 3dtr, ch5, ss) in same 2-ch sp, ss in next 2-ch sp] 6 times. *6 petals*.

Fasten off.

LEAVES (make 2 per stem)

Using C and US size B/1–C/2 (2.5mm) hook, leaving a 4in (10cm) end, ch8, ss in 2nd ch from hook, ss in next ch, 1sc in next ch, 1hdc in next ch, 1dc in next ch, 1hdc in next ch, (1sc, ch1, 1sc) in last ch, working back along opposite side of ch, 1hdc in next ch, 1dc in next ch, 1hdc in next ch, 1sc in next ch, ss in next ch.

Fasten off.

STEM (make 1 per flower head)

Cut wire to desired length allowing 2in (5cm) extra to attach to flower. Bend wire at top into small loop.

Using C and US size B/1–C/2 (2.5mm) hook, ss to base of wire, work sc around the wire to roughly midpoint (or earlier), use long end to tie leaf securely in place, pulling it tightly to ensure leaf does not flop down. Cont to sc around the wire, adding second leaf and working over leaf ends to secure them as you go.

Fasten off.

MAKING UP AND FINISHING

Sew in all yarn ends carefully.

With the RS facing outward, and using A, sew the flower head to the wire loop at the top of the stem. Bend the last 2in (5cm) of the wire and push into the bobbin.

flower power desk tidy

I love the simplicity of this little project. Each of the component pieces can be made in a single sitting, and with a color change on every round you can pick and choose to suit your mood. I like to make all the circles first just because they look pretty when I line them all up! This is a lovely "next step" project for beginners, to stretch their crochet abilities beyond the classic granny square. By practicing new stitches and patterns you overcome your limitations and move beyond them, expanding your crochet and confidence.

SKILL RATING: ● ● ●

MATERIALS:

Scheepjes Cahlista (100% cotton, approx. 92yds/85m per 1¾oz/50g ball) worsted (Aran) weight yarn
½ ball each of:
Jet Black shade 110 (MC)
Crystalline shade 385
Delphinium shade 113
Shocking Pink shade 114
Royal Orange shade 189
Yellow Gold shade 208

US size 7 (4.5mm) crochet hook

Yarn needle

10 x 14in (25 x 35cm) of black felt fabric

Sewing needle and black thread

Colorful embroidery thread

FINISHED MEASUREMENTS:

4½in (11.5cm) wide, 4½in (11.5cm) deep

GAUGE (TENSION):

Rounds 1–2 = 2½in (6.5cm) diameter, using US size 7 (4.5mm) hook.

ABBREVIATIONS:

See page 127.

FOR THE DESK TIDY

CIRCLE IN A SQUARE (make 5)

Using first color, make a magic ring, or ch6 and join with ss in first ch to form a ring.

Round 1: Ch3 (counts as first dc throughout), 11dc into the ring, join with ss in 3rd of beg 3-ch. *12 sts.*

Fasten off first color.

Round 2: Join second color in any st, ch3, 1dc in same st, 2dc in each st to end, join with ss in 3rd of beg 3-ch. *24 sts.*

Fasten off second color.

Round 3: Join third color in sp between any 2-dc group in round 2, ch3, 2dc in same sp, [skip next 2 sts, 3dc in next sp between dc] 11 times, skip last 2 sts, join with ss in 3rd of beg 3-ch. *36 sts.*

Fasten off third color.

Round 4: Join MC in sp between any 3-dc group in round 3, working in sps between 3-dc groups throughout, ch3, (2dc, ch2, 3dc) all in same sp (corner), *3hdc in each of next 2 sps, (3dc, ch2, 3dc) in next sp (corner); rep from * twice, 3hdc in each of last 2 sps, join with ss in 3rd of beg 3-ch.

Fasten off MC.

MAKING UP AND FINISHING

Place one square as the center base square and arrange the other squares with one on each side to form a cross shape. Take the base square and one side square and holding the two squares with WS together, join a contrasting color yarn into corner and ch1. Work a single crochet seam (see page 124) to join the two pieces, working through the inside loop only of each corresponding stitch. Fasten off, then repeat to join the other three squares to the sides of the base square.

Using a different colored yarn for each side seam, join each pair of adjacent squares with a single crochet seam to make an open-topped cube.

MINDFULNESS

This is a good little project if you need to take a 5-minute breather, because the small circles demand little of us beyond choosing the next color. Once you have mastered the pattern you can sit and make the circles without any thought needed, allowing your mind to gently wander as your hand guides the hook through the yarn.

ADD THE LINING

Measure the internal sides of the crochet cube and cut five squares of felt to match. Using the sewing needle and black thread, oversew (see page 124) the felt squares together to make a lining for the crochet cube. Using the sewing needle and bright embroidery thread, work 13 blanket stitches per side around the top edge of the felt cube.

Push the felt cube inside the crochet cube with WS together. Join any color yarn in corner sp of any crochet square, then work 1sc into each stitch and each blanket stitch to join the two cubes together (13 stitches per side).
Fasten off and sew in all yarn ends carefully.

- Using black as the base color really brings out the other bright shades, but you may want to work round 4 in good natural light.

prayer beads purse

This super-bright purse is made from hexagons and half hexagons, using up small scraps of yarn. Follow the layout diagram when joining the pieces as you go, to create the correct shape.

MINDFULNESS

The greatest gift from my practice of Buddhism has been the transformative experience of having and expressing gratitude. Making this purse as a gift is an act of love and generosity, as it represents many hours of crochet time and care. When we give to others it comes back to us in the form of raised self-esteem, self-worth, and happiness. Give your crochet creations to those you are grateful to, and your heart and life will expand.

SKILL RATING: ● ● ●

MATERIALS:

Scheepjes Catona (100% cotton, approx. 27yds/25m per 3/8oz 10g ball) fingering (4 ply) weight yarn

1 ball each of:

- Ultra Violet shade 282
- Jade shade 514
- Midnight shade 527
- Cyan shade 397
- Crystalline shade 385
- Lime Juice shade 392
- Yellow Gold shade 208
- Royal Orange shade 189
- Tulip shade 222
- Shocking Pink shade 114

Scheepjes Catona (100% cotton, approx. 68yds/62.5m per 7/8oz/25g ball) fingering (4 ply) weight yarn

1 ball of Bridal White shade 105 (A)

US size E/4 (3.5mm) crochet hook

Yarn needle

3/4in (2cm) button

FINISHED MEASUREMENTS:

8in (20cm) wide x 4½in (11.5cm) deep (when closed)

GAUGE (TENSION):

Rounds 1–4 of hexagon = 1¾in (4.5cm), using US size E/4 (3.5mm) hook.

ABBREVIATIONS:

See page 127.

FOR THE PURSE

Work join-as-you-go method (see page 122), following the diagram on page 109 for placement.

STARTER HEXAGON (MAKE 1)

Using any color, make a magic ring, or ch6 and join with ss in first ch to form a ring.

Round 1: Ch2 (counts as 1hdc), 11hdc into ring, join with ss in 2nd of beg 2-ch. *12 sts.*

Fasten off first color.

Round 2: Join second color in any st, ch1 (counts as first sc), 1sc in same st, ch1, skip next st, [2sc in next st, ch1, skip next st] 5 times, join with ss in beg 1-ch. *12 sts + six 1-ch sps.*

Fasten off second color.

Round 3: Join third color in any 1-ch sp, ch2 (counts as 1sc + ch1), 1sc in same sp (first corner), ch1, [(1sc, ch1, 1sc) in next 1-ch sp (for corner), ch1] 5 times, join with ss in first of beg 2-ch. *12 sts + twelve 1-ch sps.*

Fasten off third color.

Round 4: Join fourth color in any corner 1-ch sp, ch3 (counts as first sc + ch2 throughout), 1sc in same sp (first corner), [2sc in next 1-ch sp, (1sc, ch2, 1sc) in next 1-ch sp (for corner)] 5 times, 2sc in next 1-ch sp, join with ss in first of beg 3-ch.

Fasten off.

- Change color on every round throughout.

NEXT AND SUBSEQUENT HEXAGONS (make 22)

Rounds 1–3: As for starter hexagon.

Round 4: Join fourth color in any corner 1-ch sp, ch3, 1sc in same sp (first corner), 2sc in next 1-ch sp, 1sc in next corner 1-ch sp, then instead of ch2 for next corner sp, insert hook in corner sp of starting hexagon from underneath, 1sc in corner sp of starting hexagon (counts as first of 2-ch for corner sp), ch1, work second sc in corner sp of current hexagon, 1sc in next st in starter hexagon, 2sc in next 1-ch sp of current hexagon, skip next st on starter hexagon, 1sc in starter hexagon, skip next st on current hexagon, 1sc in next corner 2-ch sp on current hexagon, 1sc in corner 2-ch sp of starter hexagon, ch1, 1sc in same 2-ch sp of current hexagon.

Cont around to finish round 4 of current hexagon as normal.

Cont to join hexagons in this way throughout, according to the diagram opposite (page 109). When joining a hexagon to two previous hexagons at shared corners, join as above but replace both corner ch of current hexagon with 1sc in each adjoining hexagon.

HALF HEXAGON (make 4)

Worked in rows.

Using any color, make a magic ring.

Row 1: Ch2 (counts as 1hdc), 5hdc into ring, turn. *6 sts.*

Fasten off first color.

Row 2: Join second color in first st, ch2 (counts as 1sc throughout), 2sc in next st, [ch1, skip next st, 2sc] twice working last 2sc in 2nd of beg 2-ch from row 1, turn. *7 sts + two 1-ch sps.*

Fasten off second color.

Row 3: Join third color in first st, ch2, 1sc in st at base of 2-ch, ch1, [(1sc, ch1, 1sc) in 1-ch sp (corner), ch1] twice, 2sc in last st (2nd of beg 2-ch from prev row), turn. *8 sts + five 1-ch sps.*

Fasten off third color.

Row 4: Join fourth color in first st, ch2, 1sc in st at base of 2-ch, [2sc in next 1-ch sp, (1sc, ch2, 1sc) in next corner 1-ch sp] twice, 2sc in next 1-ch sp, 2sc in last st (2nd of beg 2-ch from prev row). *14 sts + two 2-ch sps.*

Fasten off.

DIAMOND

Worked in rows.

Using any color, make a magic ring.

Row 1: Ch2 (counts as 1hdc), 3hdc into ring, turn. *4 sts.*

Fasten off first color.

Row 2: Join second color in first st, ch2 (counts as 1sc throughout), 2sc in next st, ch1, skip next st, 2sc in last st (2nd of beg 2-ch from prev row), turn.

Fasten off second color.

Row 3: Join third color in first st, ch2, 1sc in st at base of 1-ch, ch1, (1sc, ch1, 1sc) in 1-ch sp (corner), ch1, 2sc in last st (2nd of beg 2-ch from prev row), turn.

Fasten off second color.

Row 4: Join fourth color in first st, ch2, 1sc in st at base of 1-ch, ch1, 2sc in next 1-ch sp, (1sc, ch2, 1sc) in next corner 1-ch sp (corner), 2sc in next 1-ch sp, ch1, 2sc in last st (2nd of beg 2-ch from prev row).

Fasten off.

MAKING UP AND FINISHING

Sew in all yarn ends carefully.

Sew the half hexagons into position at either end of the second and fourth rows from the bottom, using whip stitch (see page 125).

Sew the diamond between the two hexagons on the top row, with the magic ring at the top.

Lay work flat with RS facing.

BORDER

Round 1: Join A in bottom right corner hexagon on bottom row, ch1 (counts as 1sc throughout), 1sc in each of next 5 sts along side of hexagon, 1sc per row along first side of half hexagon (4 sts), 1sc in magic ring center, 1sc per row along second side of half hexagon (9 sts total along half hexagon).

Cont to work sc border around as set to diamond, work 1sc per row along first side of diamond to magic ring point (4 sts), ch5, 1sc per row along second side of diamond.

Cont to work sc border around as set to end, join with ss in beg 1-ch.

Round 2: Ch1, 1sc in each st to 5-ch at tip, 5sc in 5-ch sp, 1sc in each st to end, join with ss in beg 1-ch. Fasten off.

MAKING UP THE PURSE

With WS together, fold the piece in half aligning the bottom row to the fifth row. Using the yarn needle and A, sew the first side seam together, joining the back loops with whip stitch. Rep for the second side seam.

Turn the purse RS out and sew a button into position to fit the 5-ch buttonhole space.

christmas baubles

I'm in love with these little baubles, and when they emerged from my hook my heart skipped a beat! They make the perfect Christmas gift to give to the people we love and value in our lives. The French knot is a wonderful embellishment—and if you have yet to master it watch out, because once you do you will be placing them on everything!

MINDFULNESS

Crochet is a wonderful way to meet new like-minded people and I encourage you to seek out your local knitting and crochet group. Sharing our love of crochet with others, while hooking handmade gifts for friends or charity, expands our hearts and our lives. If you struggle with loneliness let crochet be a way of connecting with others. Never underestimate the power of the hook to bring people together.

SKILL RATING: ● ● ●

MATERIALS:

For the circles:
Rico Creative Cotton Aran (100% cotton, approx. 92yds/85m per 1¾oz/50g ball) worsted (Aran) weight yarn
Small amount each of:
Banana shade 68
Violet shade 16
Rose shade 00
Light green shade 40
Sky Blue shade 37
Candy shade 64
Tangerine shade 76
Orange shade 74
Emerald shade 69
Cardinal shade 11
Natural shade 60

For the decoration:
Anchor Artiste Metallic (80% viscose, 20% polyester, 109yds/100m per ⅞oz/25g ball) fingering (4 ply) weight yarn
Small amount of Gold shade 300

US size G/6 (4mm) crochet hook

Yarn needle

Polyester toy filling

FINISHED MEASUREMENTS:

3in (7.5cm) diameter

GAUGE (TENSION):

Rounds 1–2 = 1¾in (4.5cm) diameter, using US size G/8 (4mm) hook.

ABBREVIATIONS:

See page 127.

FOR THE BAUBLES

CIRCLE (make 3 for each bauble)

Using first color, make a magic ring, or ch6 and join with ss in first ch to form a ring.

Round 1: Ch2 (counts as first hdc throughout), 9hdc into the ring, join with ss in 2nd of beg 2-ch. *10 sts.*
Fasten off first color.

Round 2: Join second color in any st, ch2, 1hdc in same st, 2hdc in each st to end, join with ss in 2nd of first 2-ch. *20 sts.*
Fasten off second color.

Round 3: Join third color in any st, ch2, 2hdc in next st, *1hdc in next st, 2hdc in next st; rep from * to end, join with ss in 2nd of first 2-ch. *30 sts.*
Fasten off third color.

MAKING UP AND FINISHING

JOIN THE CIRCLES

Using any color and with WS tog, join yarn in any st and join 2 circles with a single crochet seam (see page 124) through the first 15 sts. Take a third circle and begin to join this to the first circle with a single crochet seam. You'll now have one circle joined to half of each of the other two. Stuff with toy filling and then continue working the single crochet seam around to close the opening. Do not fasten off, ch15, and join with a ss in the first chain to make loop to hang the bauble. Fasten off.

Sew in all yarn ends carefully.

ADD DECORATION

Using the gold yarn, work surface crochet (see page 126) around rounds 1 and 3.

Using a contrast color yarn, work surface crochet around round 2. Alternatively, using two contrasting colors alternately, make French knots (see page 123) into every other st around round 2.

techniques

In this section, we explain how to master the simple crochet and finishing techniques that you need to make the projects in this book.

Holding the hook

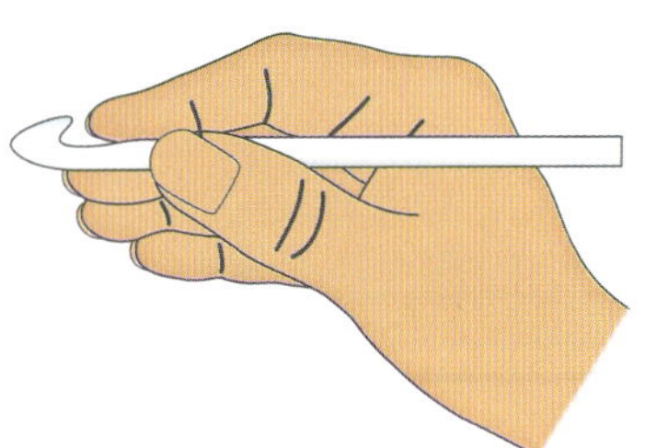

Pick up your hook as though you are picking up a pen or pencil. Keeping the hook held loosely between your fingers and thumb, turn your hand so that the palm is facing up and the hook is balanced in your hand and resting in the space between your index finger and your thumb.

You can also hold the hook like a knife—this may be easier if you are working with a large hook or with chunky yarn. Choose the method that you find most comfortable.

Holding the yarn

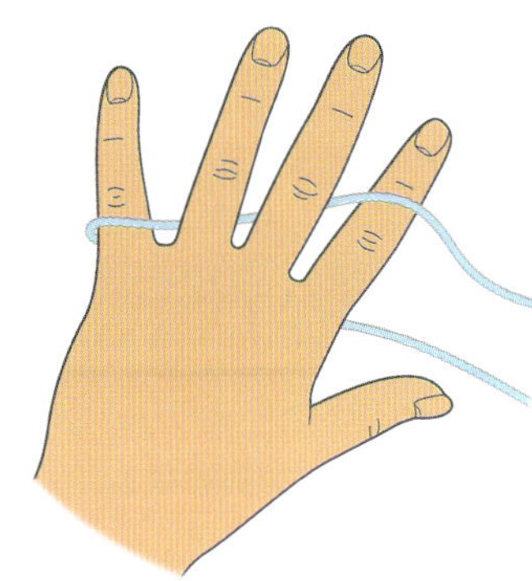

1 Pick up the yarn with your little finger in the opposite hand to your hook, with your palm facing upward and with the short end in front. Turn your hand to face downward, with the yarn on top of your index finger and under the other two fingers and wrapped right around the little finger, as shown above.

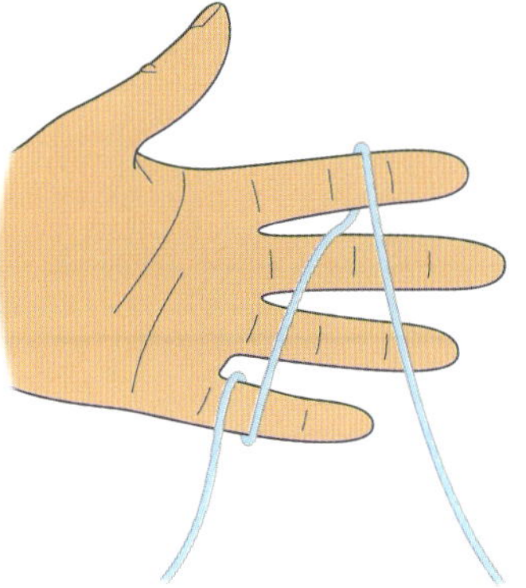

2 Turn your hand to face you, ready to hold the work in your middle finger and thumb. Keeping your index finger only at a slight curve, hold the work or the slip knot using the same hand, between your middle finger and your thumb and just below the crochet hook and loop/s on the hook.

Making a slip knot

The simplest way is to make a circle with the yarn, so that the loop is facing downward.

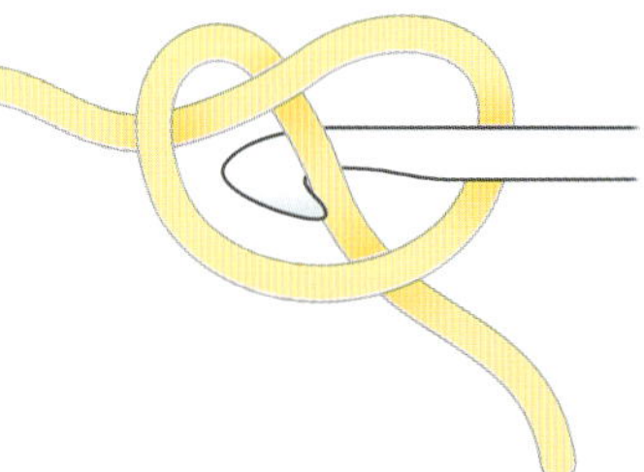

1 In one hand hold the circle at the top where the yarn crosses, and let the end drop down at the back so that it falls across the center of the loop. With your free hand or the tip of a crochet hook, pull a loop through the circle.

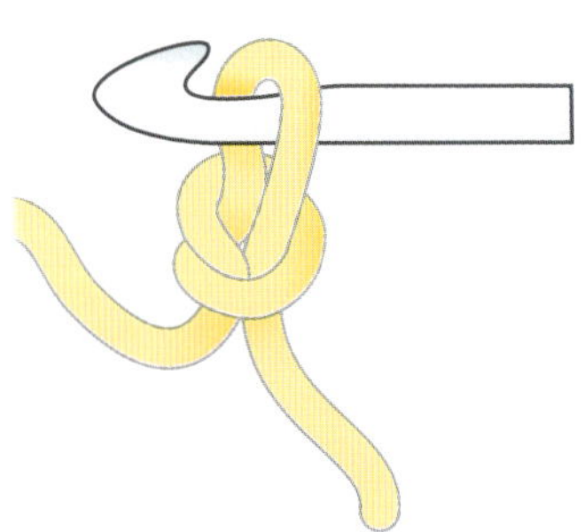

2 Put the hook into the loop and pull gently so that it forms a loose loop on the hook.

Yarn over hook (yo)

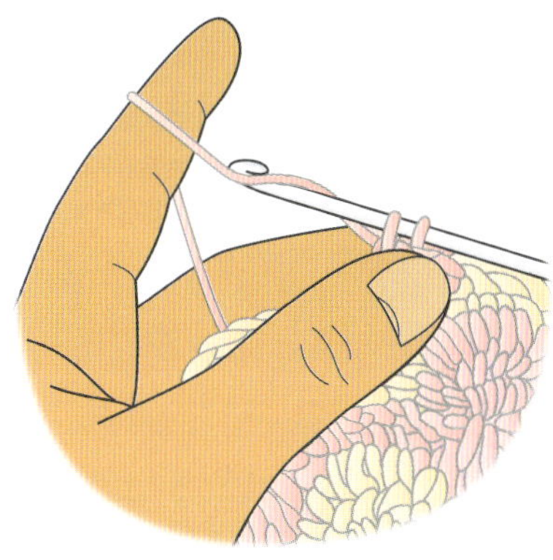

To create a stitch, catch the yarn from behind with the hook pointing upward. As you gently pull the yarn through the loop on the hook, turn the hook so it faces downward and slide the yarn through the loop. The loop on the hook should be kept loose enough for the hook to slide through easily.

Magic ring

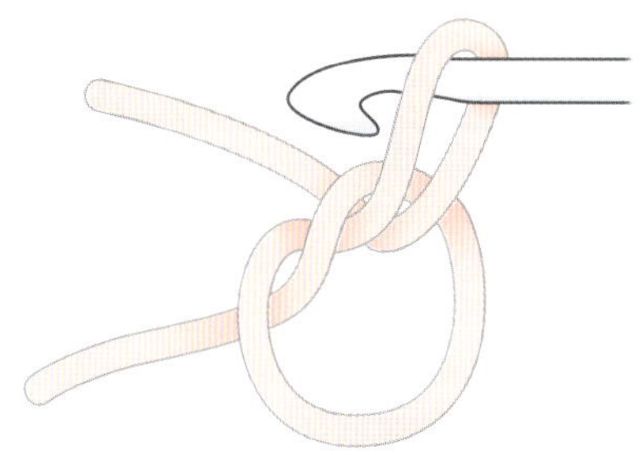

This is a useful starting technique if you do not want a visible hole in the center of your round. Loop the yarn around your finger, insert the hook through the ring, yarn over hook, pull through the ring to make the first chain. Work the number of stitches required into the ring and then pull the end to tighten the center ring and close the hole.

Chain (ch)

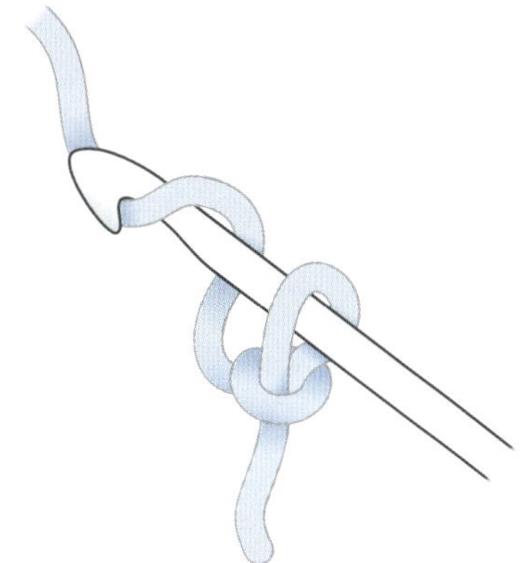

1 Using the hook, wrap the yarn over the hook ready to pull it through the loop on the hook.

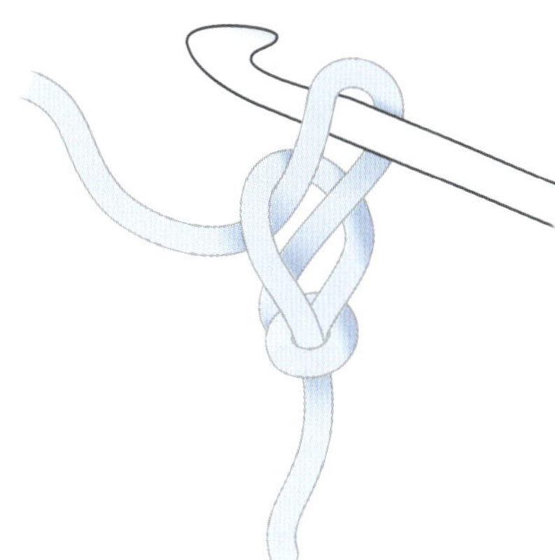

2 Pull through, creating a new loop on the hook. Continue in this way to create a chain of the required length.

Chain ring

If you are crocheting a round shape, one way of starting off is by crocheting a number of chains following the instructions in your pattern, and then joining them into a circle.

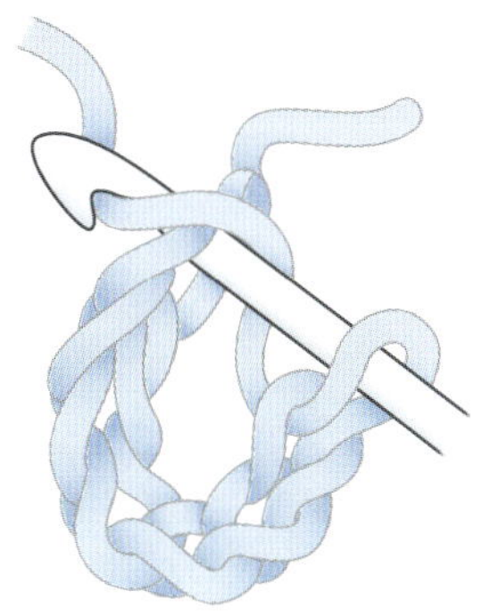

1 To join the chain into a circle, insert the crochet hook into the first chain that you made (not into the slip knot), yarn over hook.

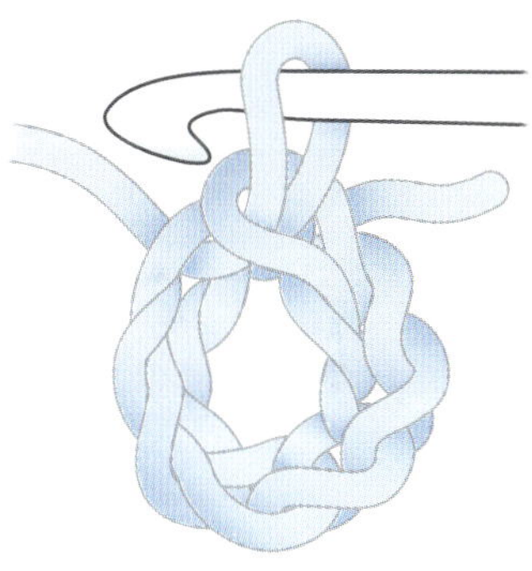

2 Pull the yarn through the chain and through the loop on your hook at the same time, thereby creating a slip stitch and forming a circle. You now have a chain ring ready to work stitches into as instructed in the pattern.

Chain space (ch sp)

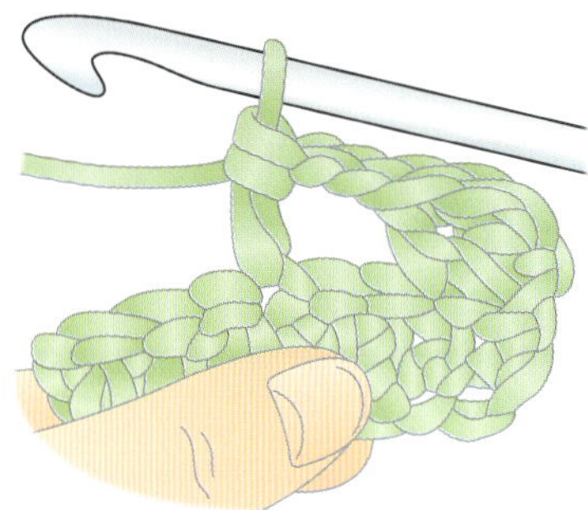

1 A chain space is the space that has been made under a chain in the previous round or row, and falls in between other stitches.

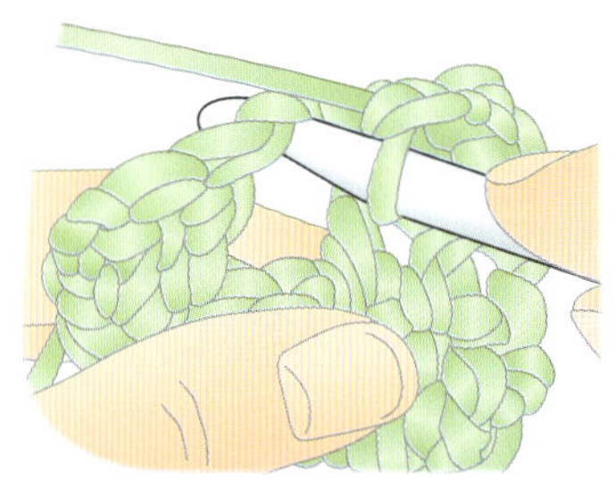

2 Stitches into a chain space are made directly into the hole created under the chain and not into the chain stitches themselves.

Slip stitch (ss)

A slip stitch doesn't create any height and is often used as the last stitch to create a smooth and even round or row.

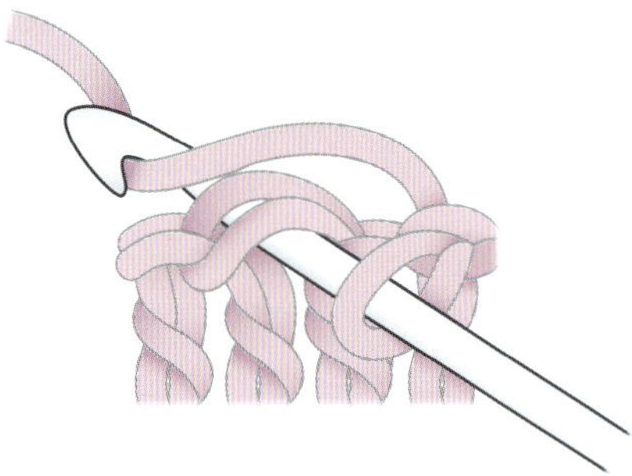

1 To make a slip stitch: first put the hook through the work, yarn over hook.

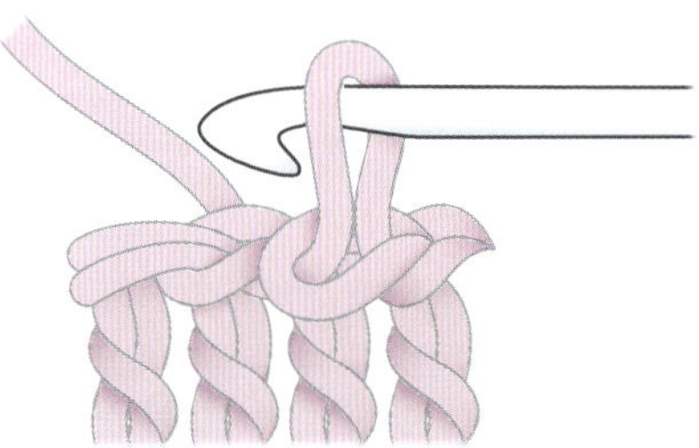

2 Pull the yarn through both the work and through the loop on the hook at the same time, so you will have 1 loop on the hook.

Making rounds

When working in rounds the work is not turned, so you are always working from one side. Depending on the pattern you are working, a "round" can be square. Start each round by making one or more chains to create the height you need for the stitch you are working:
Single crochet = 1 chain
Half double crochet = 2 chains
Double crochet = 3 chains
Treble = 4 chains
Work the required stitches to complete the round. At the end of the round, slip stitch into the top of the chain to close the round.

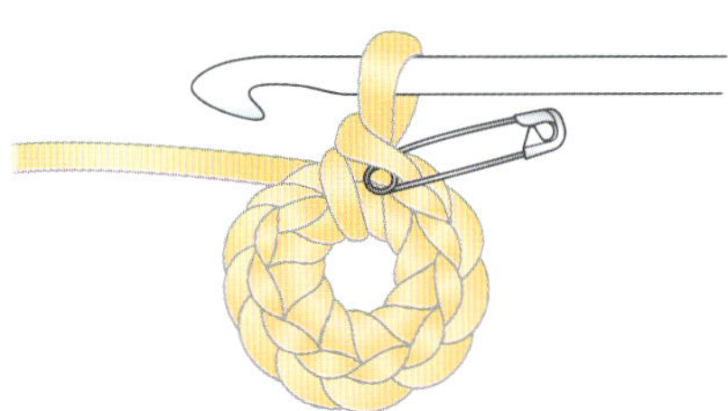

If you work in a spiral you do not need a turning chain. After completing the base ring, place a stitch marker in the first stitch and then continue to crochet around. When you have made a round and reached the point where the stitch marker is, work this stitch, take out the stitch marker from the previous round and put it back into the first stitch of the new round. A safety pin or piece of yarn in a contrasting color makes a good stitch marker.

Making rows

When making straight rows you turn the work at the end of each row and make a turning chain to create the height you need for the stitch you are working with, as for making rounds.
Single crochet = 1 chain
Half double crochet = 2 chains
Double crochet = 3 chains
Treble = 4 chains

Working into top of stitch

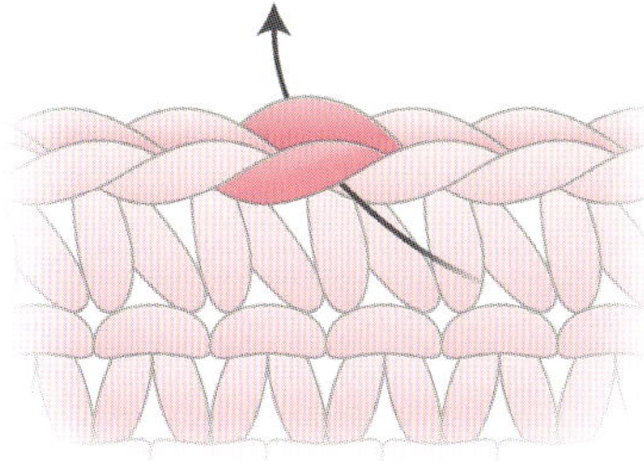

Unless otherwise directed, always insert the hook under both of the two loops on top of the stitch—this is the standard technique.

Working into front loop of stitch (FLO)

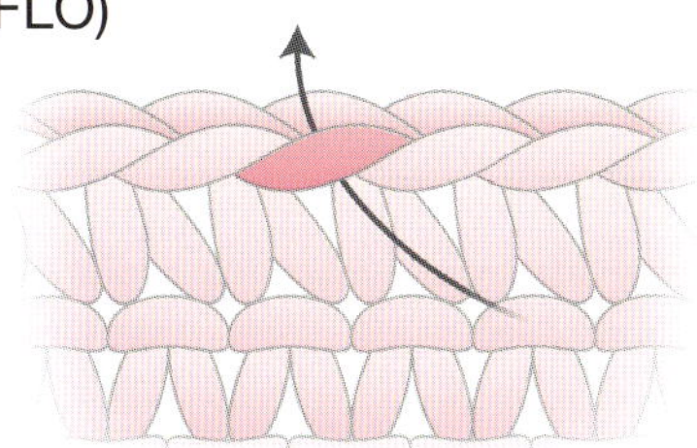

To work into the front loop of a stitch, pick up the front loop from underneath at the front of the work.

Working into back loop of stitch (BLO)

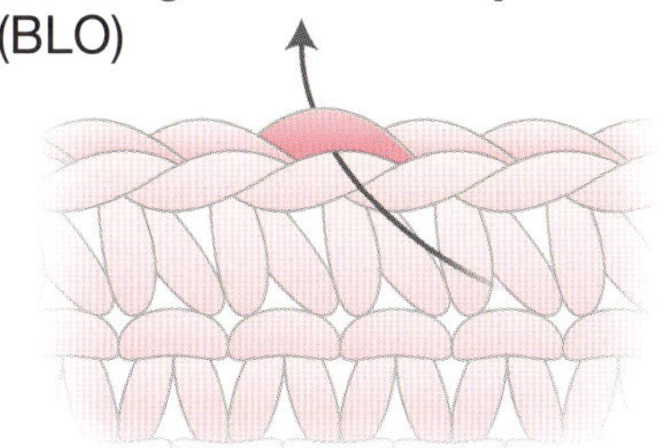

To work into the back loop of the stitch, insert the hook between the front and the back loop, picking up the back loop from the front of the work.

How to measure a gauge (tension) square

Using the hook and the yarn recommended in the pattern, make a number of chains to measure approximately 6in (15cm). Working in the stitch pattern given for the gauge (tension) measurements, work enough rows to form a square. Fasten off.
Take a ruler, place it horizontally across the square and, using pins, mark a 4in (10cm) area. Repeat vertically to form a 4in (10cm) square on the fabric.
Count the number of stitches across, and the number of rows within the square, and compare against the gauge (tension) given in the pattern.

If your numbers match the pattern then use this size hook and yarn for your project. If you have more stitches, then your gauge (tension) is tighter than recommended and you need to use a larger hook. If you have fewer stitches, then your gauge (tension) is looser and you will need a smaller hook.
Make gauge (tension) squares using different size hooks until you have matched that given in the pattern, and use this hook to make the project.

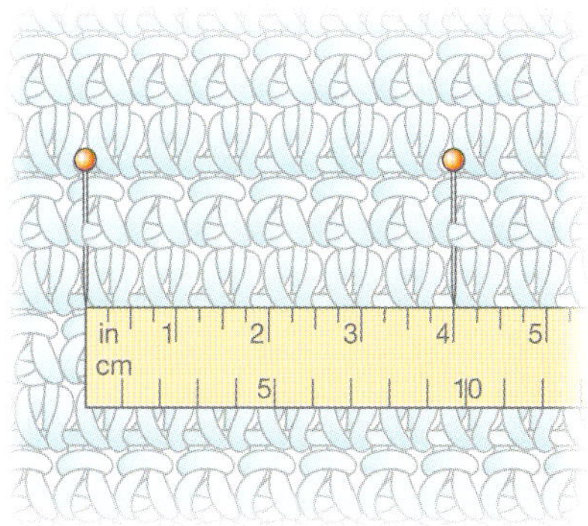

Single crochet (sc)

1 Insert the hook into your work, yarn over hook and pull the yarn through the work only. You will then have 2 loops on the hook.

2 Yarn over hook again and pull through the two loops on the hook. You will then have 1 loop on the hook.

Half double crochet (hdc)

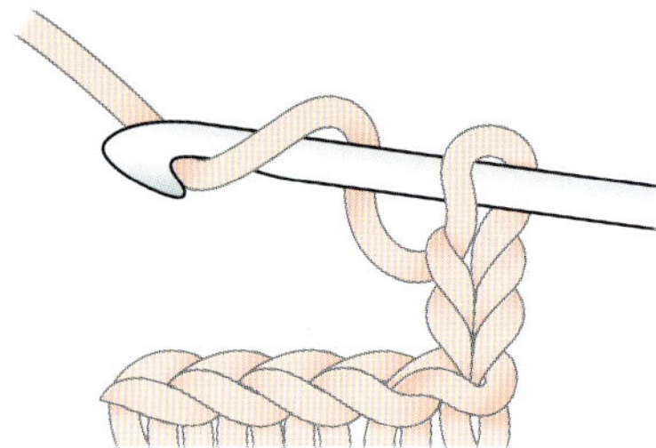

1 Before inserting the hook into the work, wrap the yarn over the hook and put the hook through the work with the yarn wrapped around.

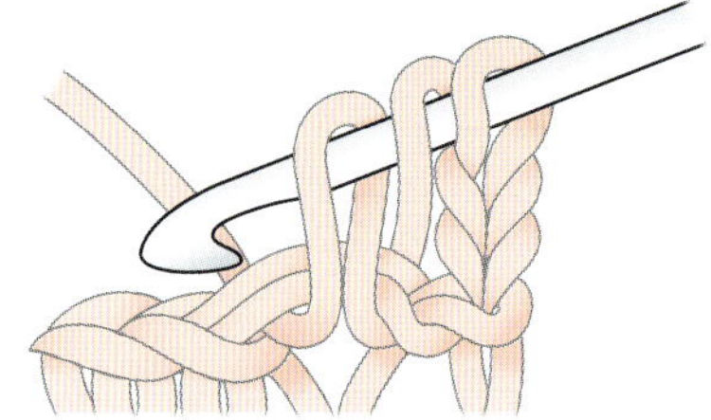

2 Yarn over hook again and pull through the first loop on the hook. You now have 3 loops on the hook.

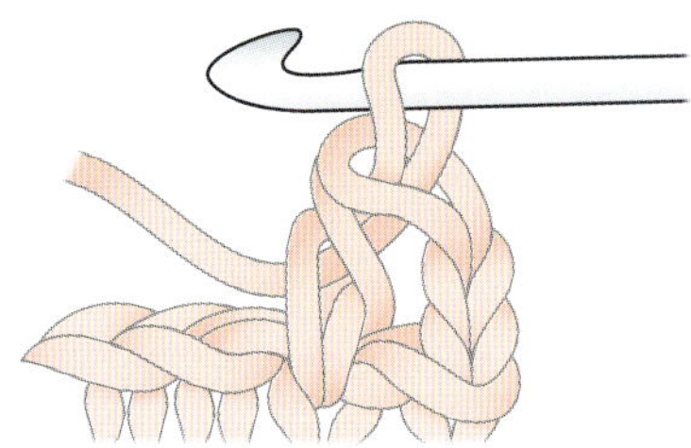

3 Yarn over hook and pull the yarn through all 3 loops. You will be left with 1 loop on the hook.

Double crochet (dc)

1 Before inserting the hook into the work, wrap the yarn over the hook. Put the hook through the work with the yarn wrapped around, yarn over hook again and pull through the first loop on the hook. You now have 3 loops on the hook.

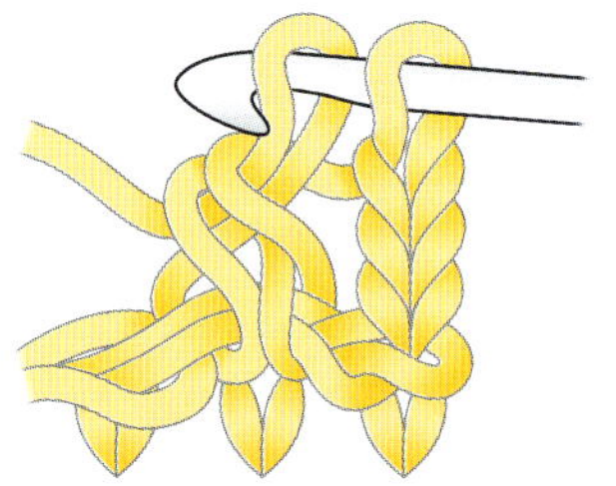

2 Yarn over hook again, pull the yarn through the first 2 loops on the hook. You now have 2 loops on the hook.

3 Pull the yarn through 2 loops again. You will be left with 1 loop on the hook.

Treble (tr)

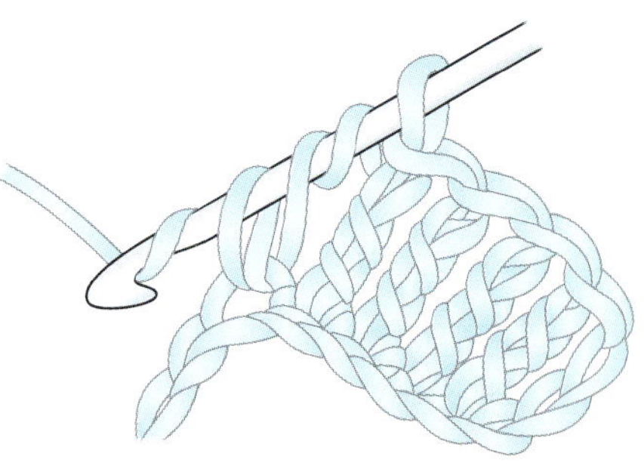

Yarn over hook twice, insert the hook into the stitch, yarn over hook, pull a loop through (4 loops on hook), yarn over hook, pull the yarn through 2 stitches (3 loops on hook), yarn over hook, pull a loop through the next 2 stitches (2 loops on hook), yarn over hook, pull a loop through the last 2 stitches. You will be left with 1 loop on the hook.

Double treble (dtr)

Double trebles are "tall" stitches and are an extension on the basic double crochet stitch. They need a turning chain of 5 chains.

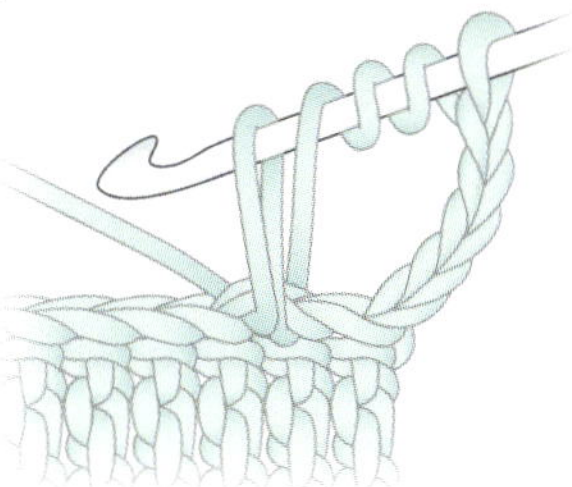

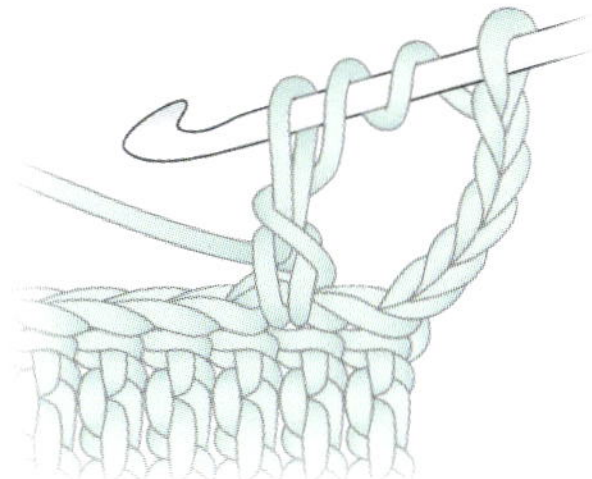

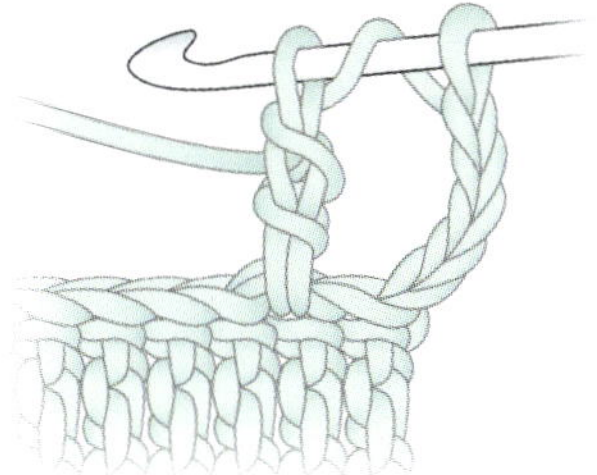

1 Yarn over hook three times, insert the hook into the stitch or space. Yarn over hook, pull the yarn through the work (5 loops on hook).

2 Yarn over hook, pull the yarn through the first 2 loops on the hook (4 loops on hook).

3 Yarn over hook, pull the yarn through the first 2 loops on the hook (3 loops on hook).

4 Yarn over hook, pull the yarn through the first 2 loops on the hook (2 loops on hook). Yarn over hook, pull the yarn through the 2 loops on the hook. You will be left with 1 loop on the hook.

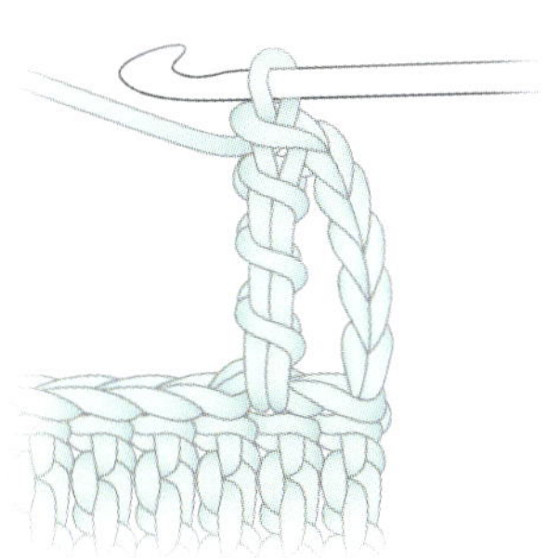

Elongated single crochet (esc)

This stitch is also sometimes called long single crochet or spike stitch. You just work an ordinary single crochet stitch, but into the stitch that's one, two or more rows below, which creates a V of yarn on the surface. These instructions are for an esc worked into the top of the stitch 2 rows below.

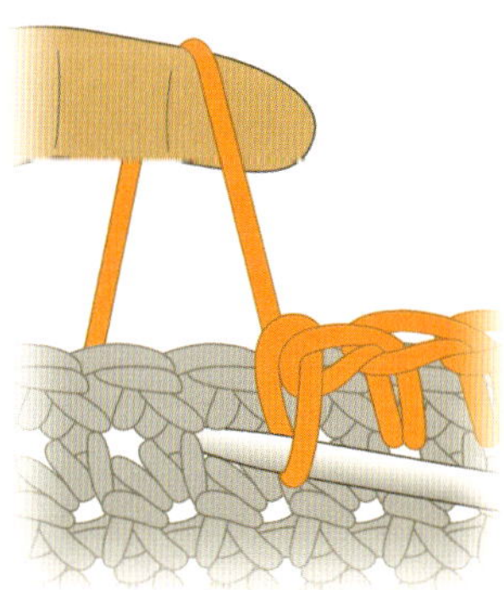

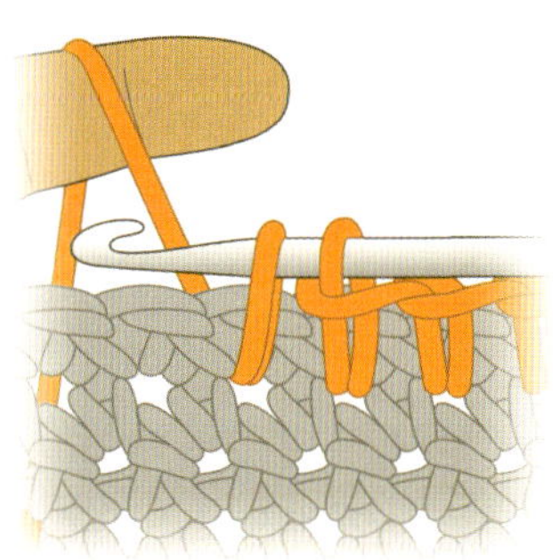

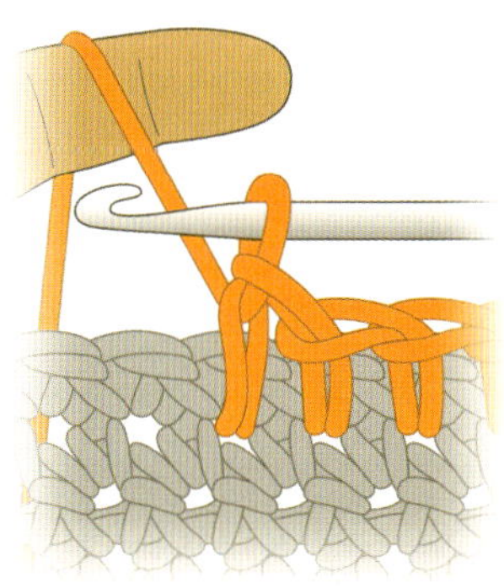

1 Using a contrast yarn, insert your hook into the space one row below the next stitch—this is the top of the stitch one row below, so the same place that the stitch in the previous row is worked.

2 Yarn over hook and draw a loop up so it's level with the original loop on your hook.

3 Yarn over hook and pull through both loops to complete the elongated single crochet.

Front post double crochet (FPdc)

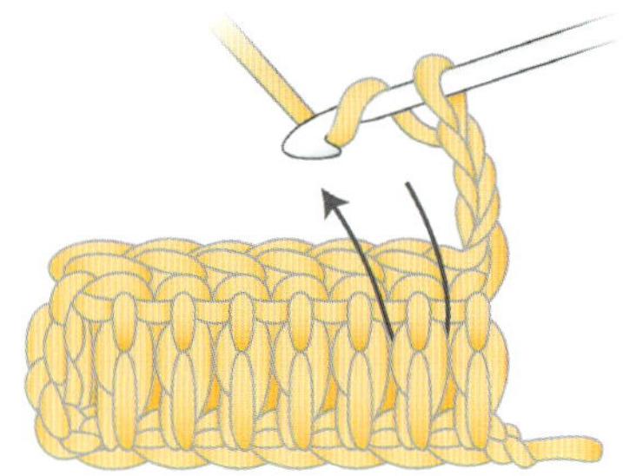

1 Yarn over hook and insert the hook from the front and around the post (the stem) of the next double crochet from right to left.

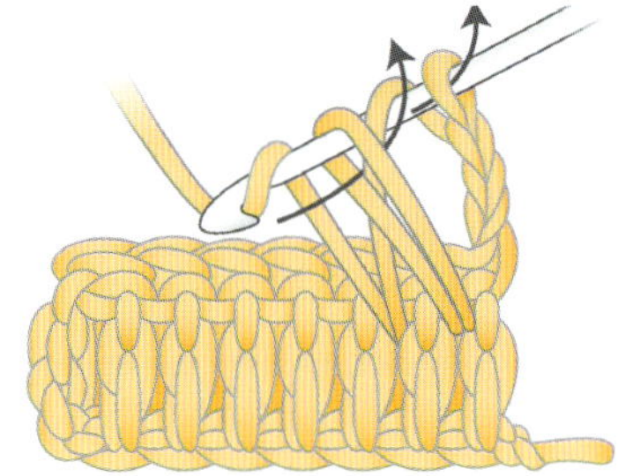

2 Yarn over hook and pull the yarn through the work, yarn over hook and pull the yarn through the first 2 loops on the hook.

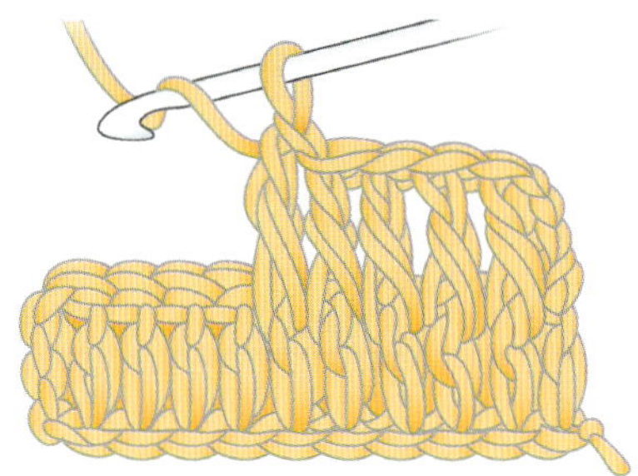

3 Yarn over hook and pull the yarn through the 2 loops on the hook (1 loop on hook). One front post double crochet completed.

Back post double crochet (BPdc)

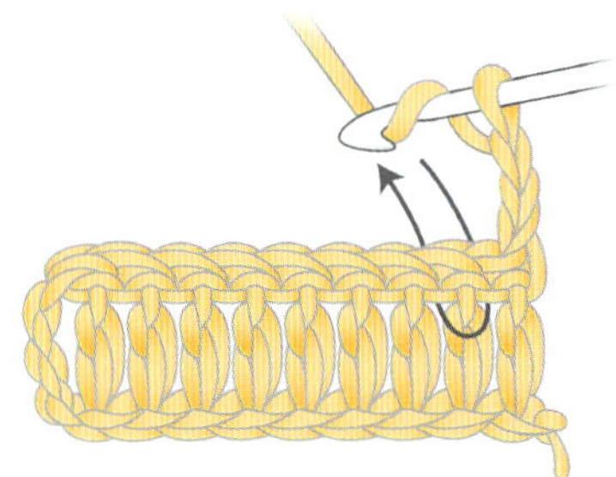

1 Yarn over hook and insert the hook from the back and around the post (the stem) of the next double crochet as directed in the pattern from right to left.

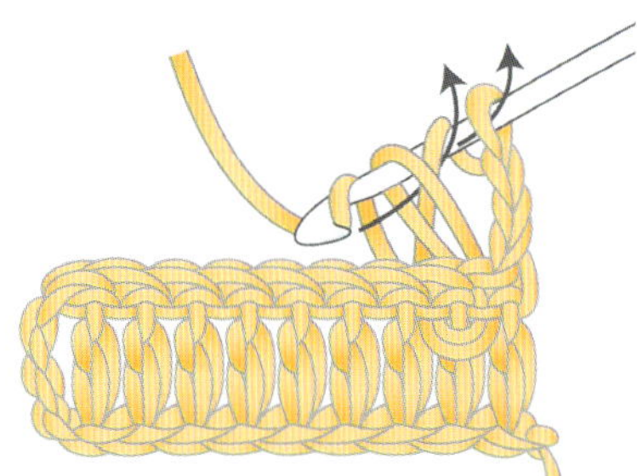

2 Yarn over hook and pull the yarn through the work, yarn over hook and pull the yarn through the first 2 loops on the hook.

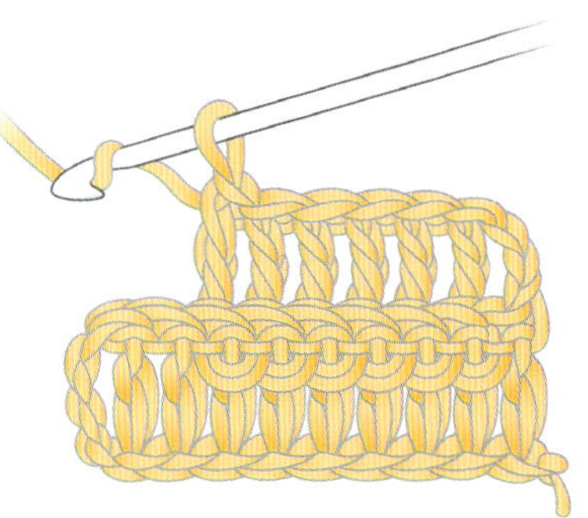

3 Yarn over hook and pull the yarn through the 2 loops on the hook (1 loop on hook). One back post double crochet completed.

Popcorn stitch (PC)

This example shows a popcorn made with four double crochet stitches worked into a foundation chain, but a popcorn can be worked into any stitch or space and can be made up of any practical number or combination of stitches.

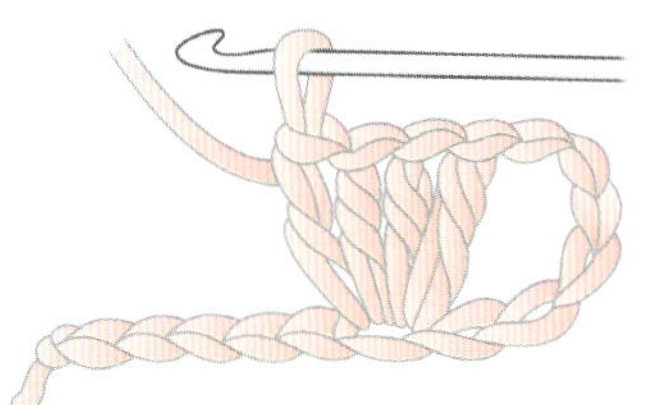

1 Inserting the hook in the same place each time, work four complete double crochet stitches.

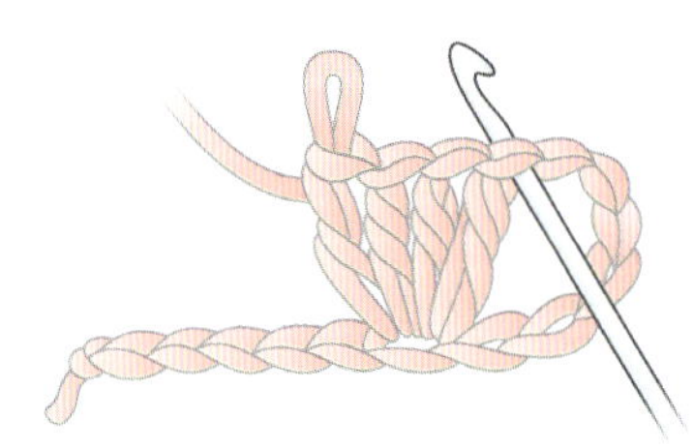

2 Slip the hook out of the last loop and insert it into the top of the first stitch.

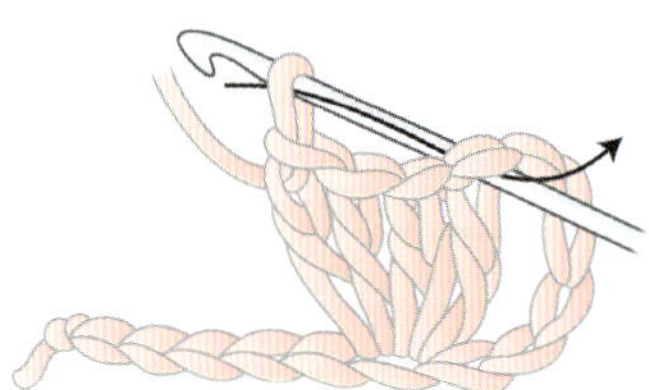

3 Then insert the hook into the loop of the last stitch again. Yarn over hook and pull it through as indicated.

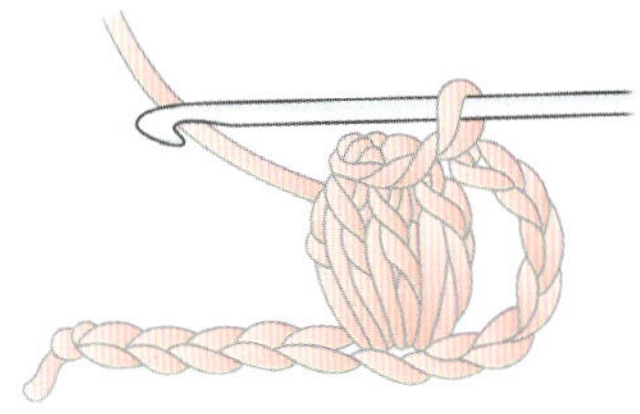

4 This makes one complete popcorn.

Clusters (cl)

Clusters are groups of stitches, with each stitch only partly worked and then all joined at the end to form one stitch that creates a particular pattern and shape. They are most effective when made using a longer stitch such as a double crochet. Shown here is a three-double crochet cluster, but for four- or five-double crochet clusters, simply repeat steps 1 and 2 more times.

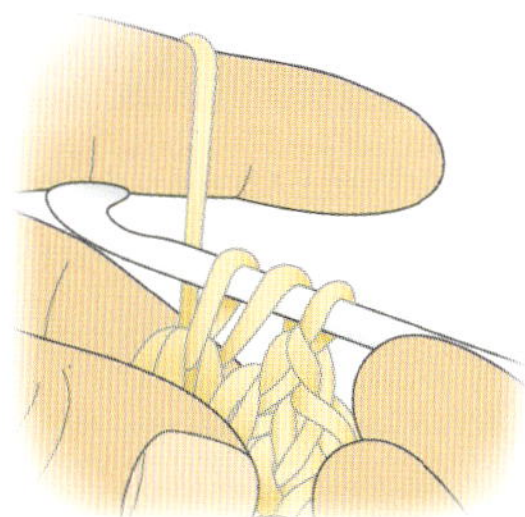

1 Yarn over hook, insert the hook in the stitch (or space). Yarn over hook, pull the yarn through the work (3 loops on hook).

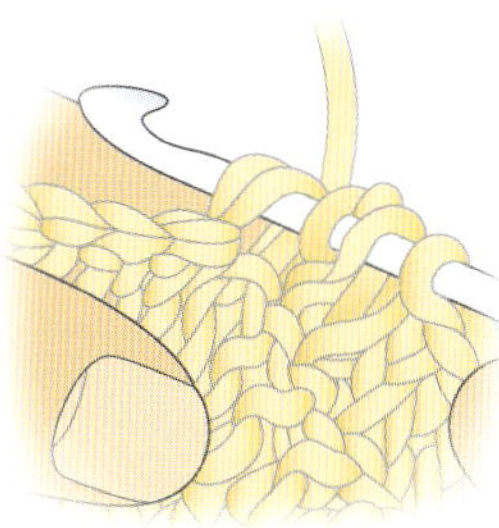

2 Yarn over hook, pull the yarn through 2 of the loops on the hook. Yarn over hook, insert the hook in the same stitch (or space).

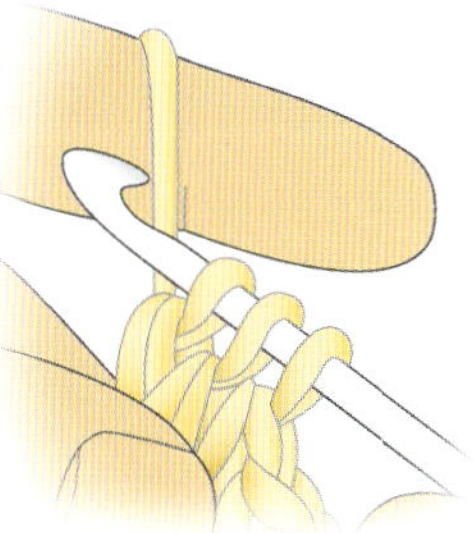

3 Yarn over hook, pull the yarn through the work (4 loops on hook). Yarn over hook, pull the yarn through 2 of the loops on the hook (3 loops on hook).

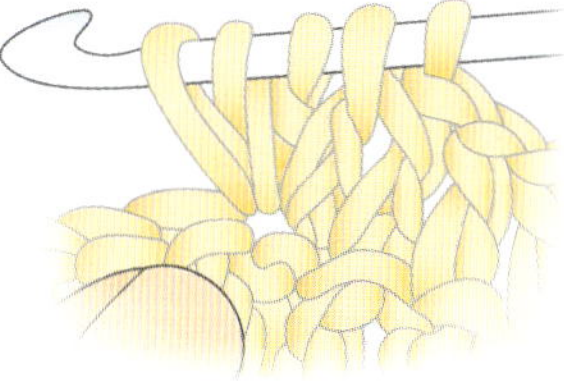

4 Yarn over hook, insert the hook in the same stitch (or space), yarn over hook, pull the yarn through the work (5 loops on hook).

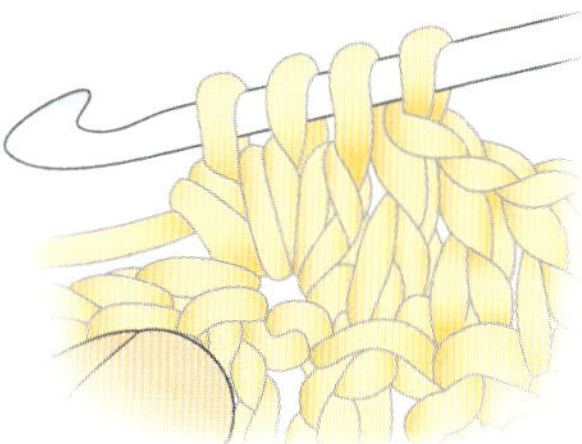

5 Yarn over hook, pull the yarn through 2 of the loops on the hook (4 loops on hook).

6 Yarn over hook, pull the yarn through all 4 loops on the hook (1 loop left on hook). One three-double crochet cluster made.

Puff stitch (PS)

A puff stitch is a padded stitch worked by creating several loops on the hook before completing the stitch. The basic principle is always the same, but you can repeat steps 1 and 2 fewer times to make a smaller puff. Sometimes a chain is worked at the end to secure the puff.

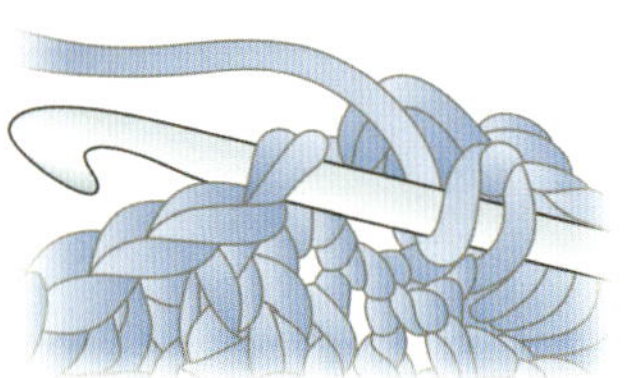

1 Yarn over hook, and insert the hook into the next stitch or space.

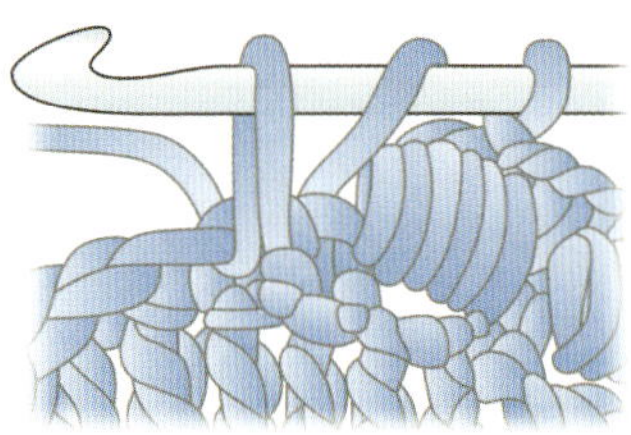

2 Yarn over hook again and draw through, keeping the loops of yarn long.

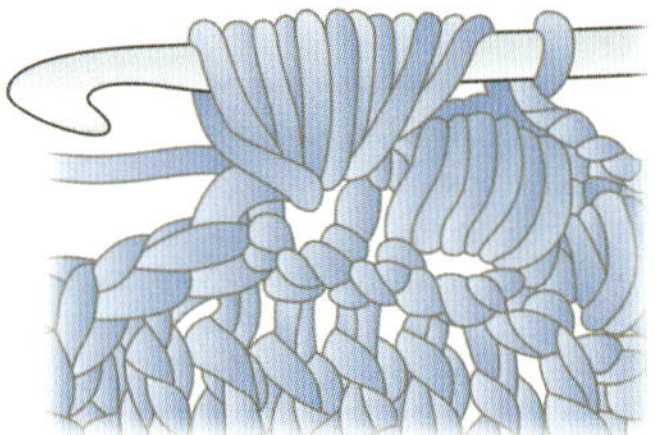

3 Repeat steps 1 and 2 five more times, keeping the loops long each time. There will be 13 loops on the hook.

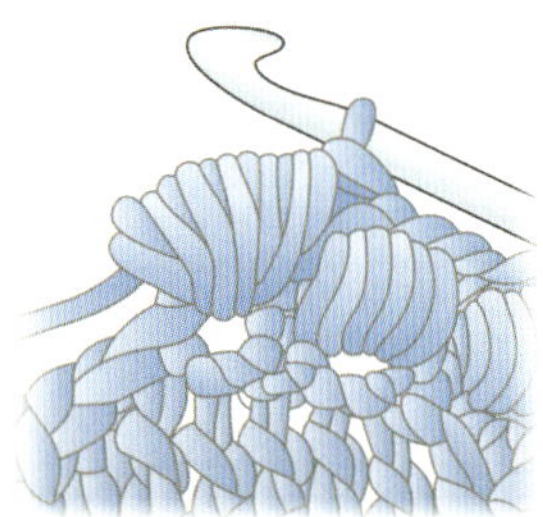

4 Yarn over hook and draw through all the loops on the hook.

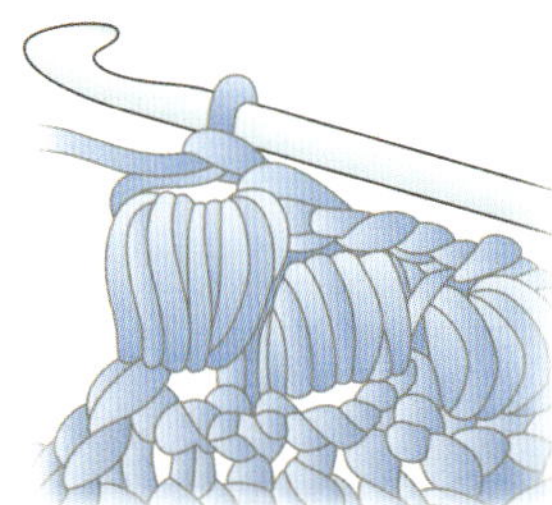

5 Yarn over hook, and draw through the single loop on the hook to make a chain and secure the puff stitch.

Increasing

Make two or three stitches into one stitch or space from the previous row. The illustration shows a double crochet increase being made.

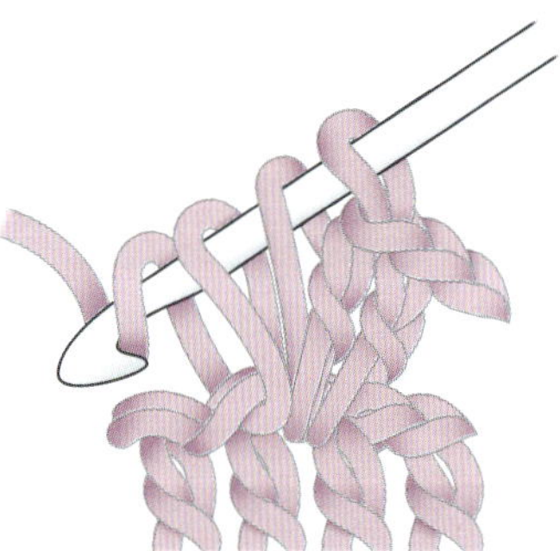

Decreasing

You can decrease by either missing the next stitch and continuing to crochet, or by crocheting two or more stitches together. The basic technique for crocheting stitches together is the same, no matter which stitch you are using. The following example shows sc2tog.

SINGLE CROCHET TWO STITCHES TOGETHER (sc2tog)

1 Insert the hook into your work, yarn over hook and pull the yarn through the work (2 loops on hook). Insert the hook in next stitch, yarn over hook and pull the yarn through.

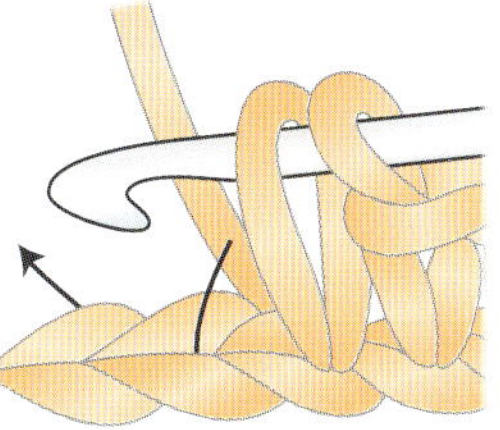

2 Yarn over hook again and pull through all 3 loops on the hook. You will then have 1 loop on the hook.

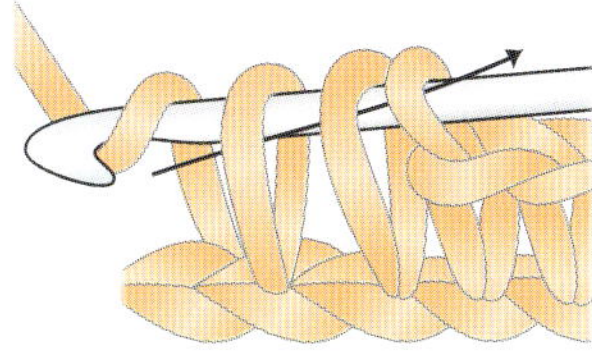

Joining yarn at the end of a row or round

You can use this technique when changing color, or when joining in a new ball of yarn as one runs out.

1 Keep the loop of the old yarn on the hook. Drop the end and catch a loop of the strand of the new yarn with the crochet hook.

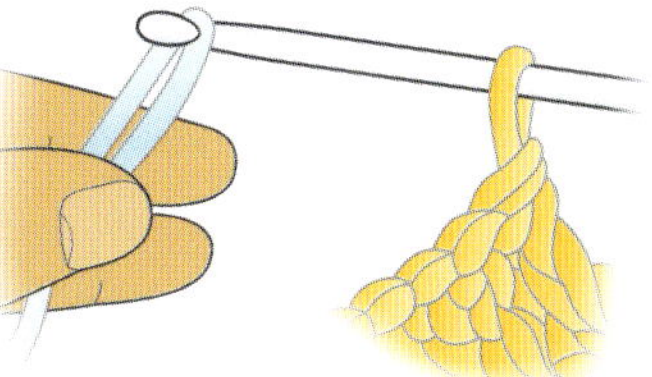

2 Draw the new yarn through the loop on the hook, keeping the old loop drawn tight and continue as instructed in the pattern.

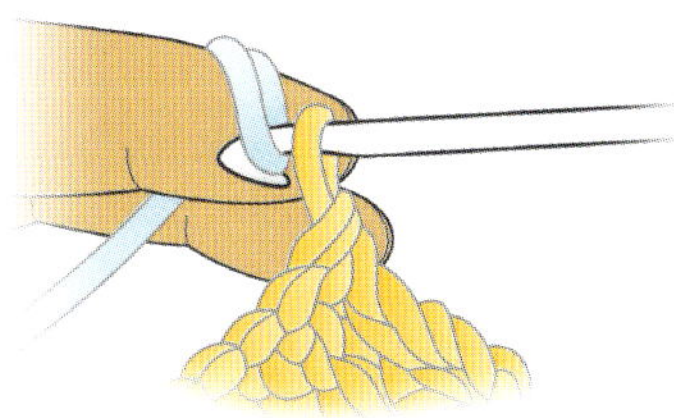

Joining in new yarn after fastening off

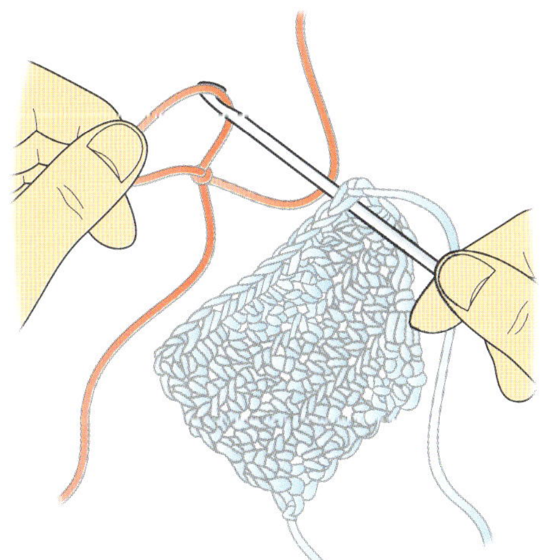

1 Fasten off the old color (see page 123). Make a slip knot with the new color (see page 112). Insert the hook into the stitch at the beginning of the next row, then through the slip knot.

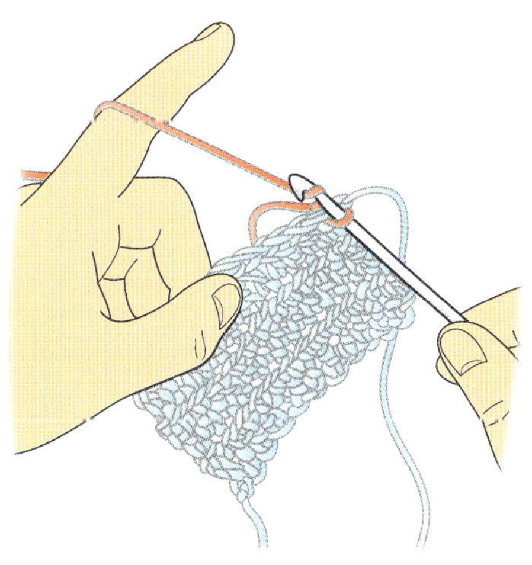

2 Draw the loop of the slip knot through to the front of the work. Carry on working using the new color, following the instructions in the pattern.

Joining yarn in the middle of a row or round

For a neat color join in the middle of a row or round, use these methods.

JOINING A NEW COLOR INTO SINGLE CROCHET

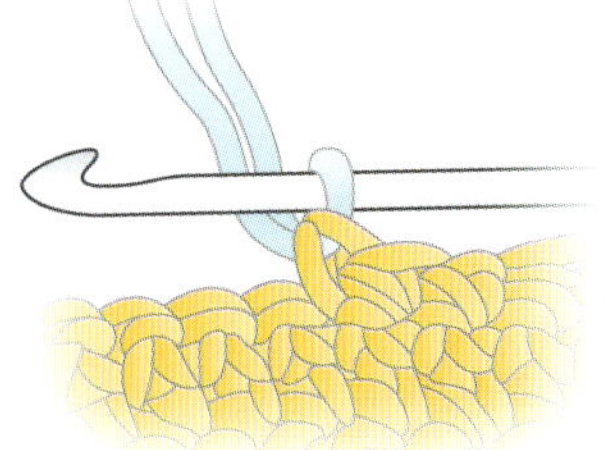

1 Make a single crochet stitch (see page 115), but do not draw the final loop through, so there are 2 loops on the hook. Drop the old yarn, catch the new yarn with the hook and draw it through both loops to complete the stitch and join in the new color at the same time.

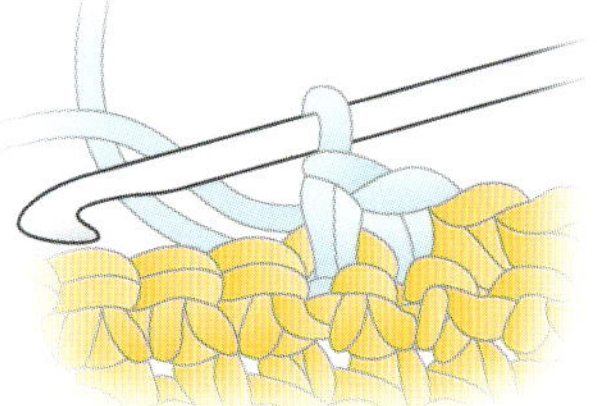

2 Continue to crochet with the new yarn. Cut the old yarn leaving a 6in (15cm) endl and weave the end in (see right) after working a row, or once the work is complete.

JOINING A NEW COLOR INTO DOUBLE CROCHET

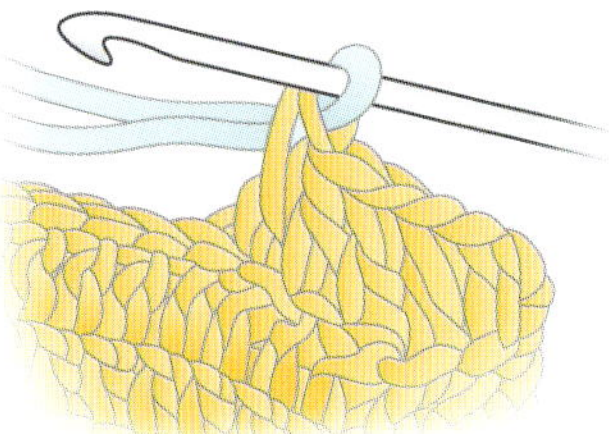

1 Make a double crochet stitch (see page 116), but do not draw the final loop through, so there are 2 loops on the hook. Drop the old yarn, catch the new yarn with the hook and draw it through both loops to complete the stitch and join in the new color at the same time.

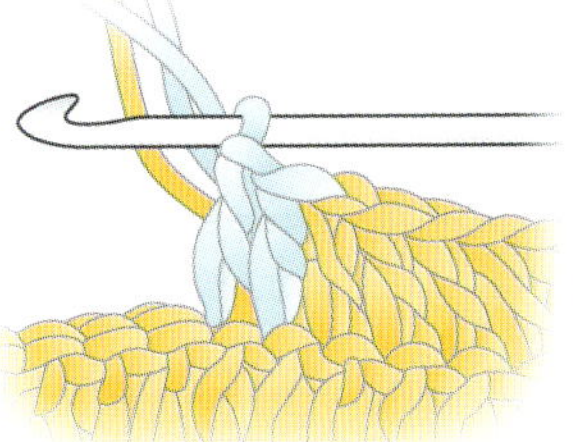

2 Continue to crochet with the new yarn. Cut the old yarn leaving a 6in (15cm) end and weave the end in (see right) after working a row, or once the work is complete.

Join-as-you-go method

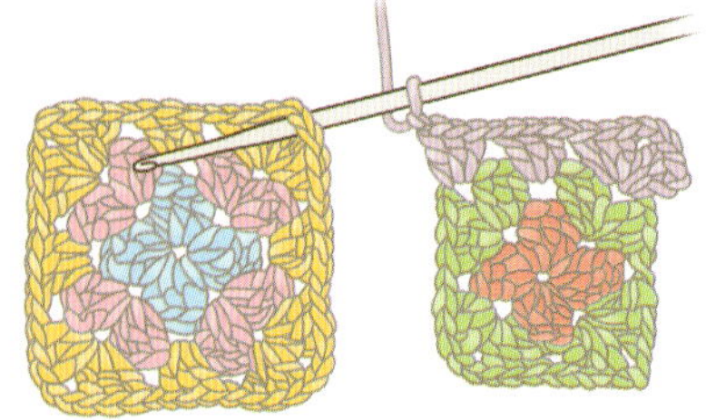

1 Work the first side of the current square including the first corner grouping (first set of 3hdc or 3dc), then instead of making ch2 for the corner space, insert the hook into the corner space of the starting square from underneath as shown.

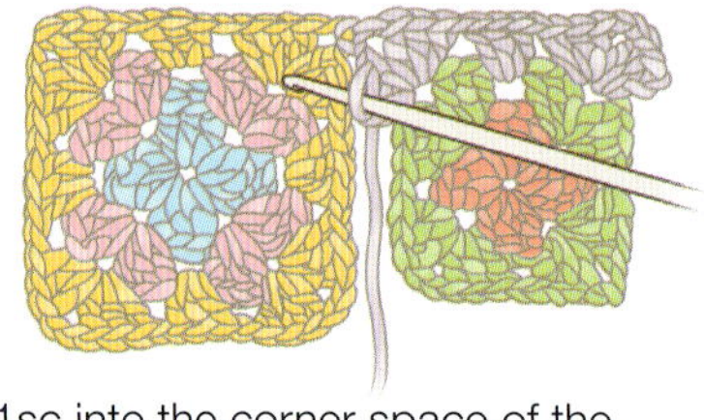

2 1sc into the corner space of the starting square (counts as first of 2-ch for the corner space), ch1, then work the second 3hdc or 3dc grouping into the corner space of the current square as usual.

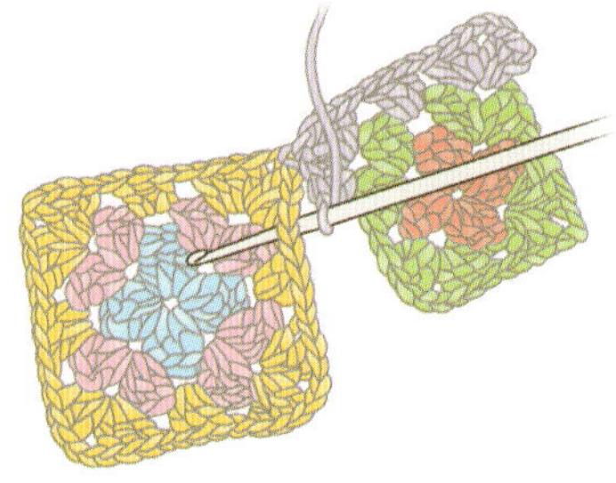

3 To continue joining the squares together, instead of ch1, work 1sc into the next side space of the starting square.

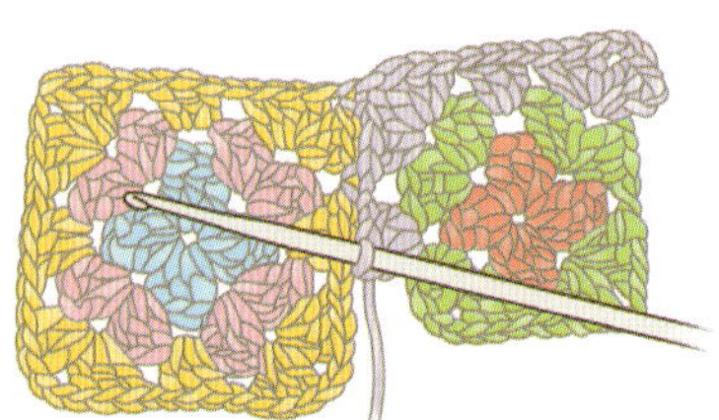

4 3hdc or 3dc in the next side space of the current square. Continue replacing each ch1 at the side of the current square with 1sc in the next side space of the starting square, and replacing the first of the ch-2 at the corner space of the current square with 1dc in the corner space of the starting square.

5 When the current square is joined to the starting square along one side, continue around and finish the final round of the current square as normal.

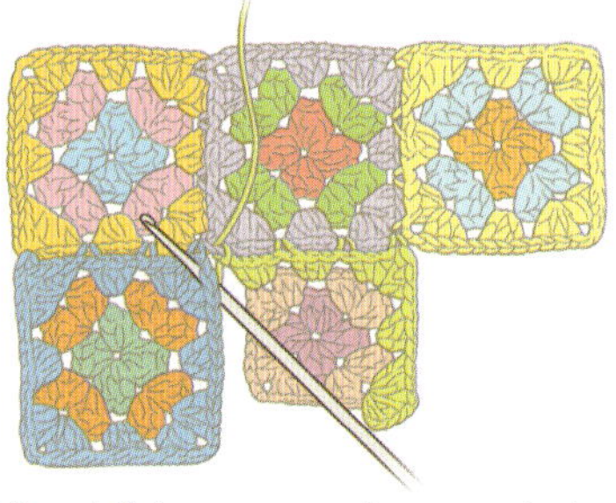

6 When joining a current square to two previous squares, replace both corner ch of the current square with 1sc into each adjoining square.

Enclosing a yarn end

You may find that the yarn end gets in the way as you work; you can enclose this into the stitches as you go by placing the end at the back as you wrap the yarn. This also saves having to sew this yarn end in later.

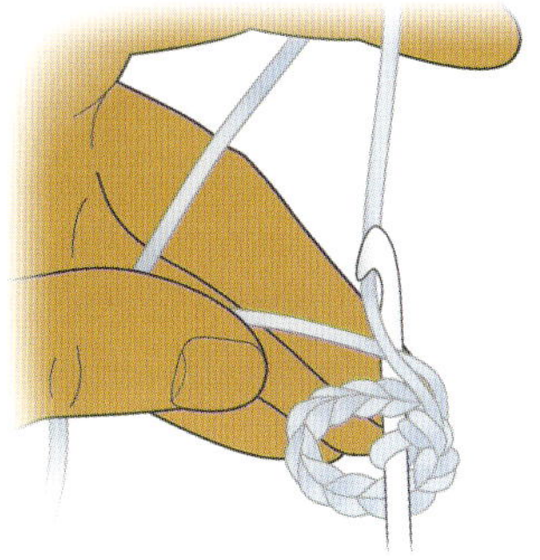

Fastening off

When you have finished crocheting, you need to fasten off the stitches to stop all your work unravelling.

1 Draw up the final loop of the last stitch to make it bigger. Cut the yarn, leaving an end of approximately 4in (10cm)—unless a longer end is needed for sewing up. Pull the end all the way through the loop and pull the loop up tightly.

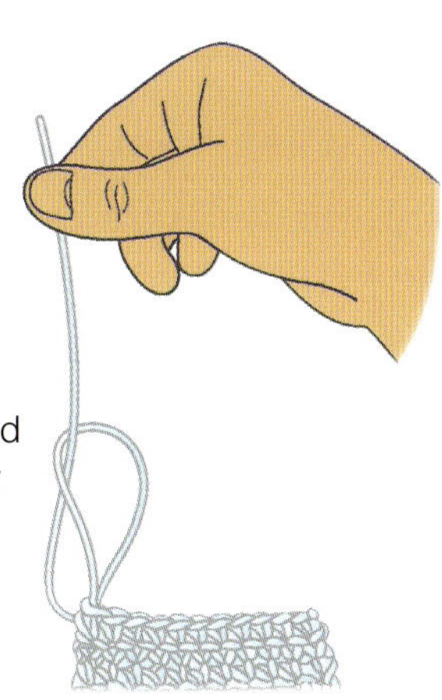

Weaving in yarn ends

It is important to weave in the ends of the yarn so that they are secure and your crochet won't unravel. Thread a yarn needle with the yarn end. On the wrong side, take the needle through the crochet one stitch down on the edge, then take it through the stitches, working in a gentle zig-zag. Work through four or five stitches then return in the opposite direction. Remove the needle, pull the crochet gently to stretch it and trim the end.

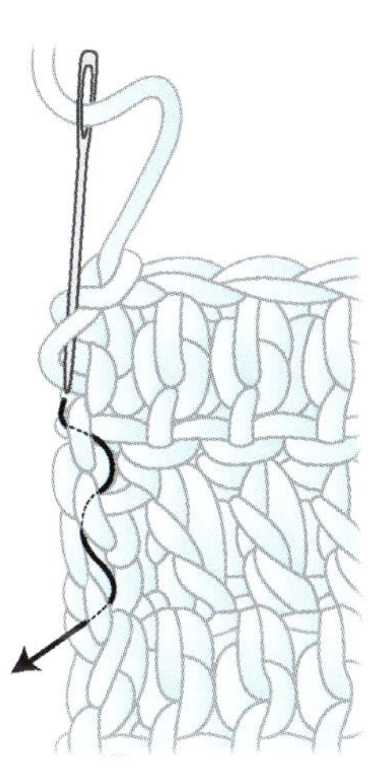

Making a French knot

Bring the needle up from the back of the fabric to the front. Wrap the thread two or three times around the tip of the needle, then reinsert the needle at the point where it first emerged, holding the wrapped threads with the thumbnail of your non-stitching hand, and pull the needle all the way through. The wraps will form a knot on the surface of the fabric.

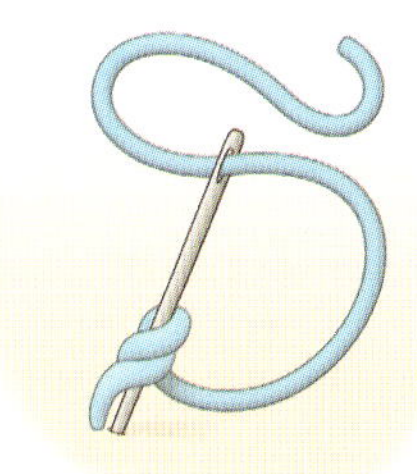

Blocking

When making some of the projects, such as garlands or mandalas, you will find that taking the time to block and stiffen each crochet element will make a huge difference to the finished effect of your work. Without either of these processes you will find that the crochet will curl out of shape and lose its definition.

For a quick and easy way to block your crochet you'll need blocking pins, some soft foam mats (such as the ones sold as children's play mats) and some ironing spray starch. Pin each item out to shape and size onto the mats and then spray with the starch. Allow to dry for a day before attaching the elements to your garland or mandala.

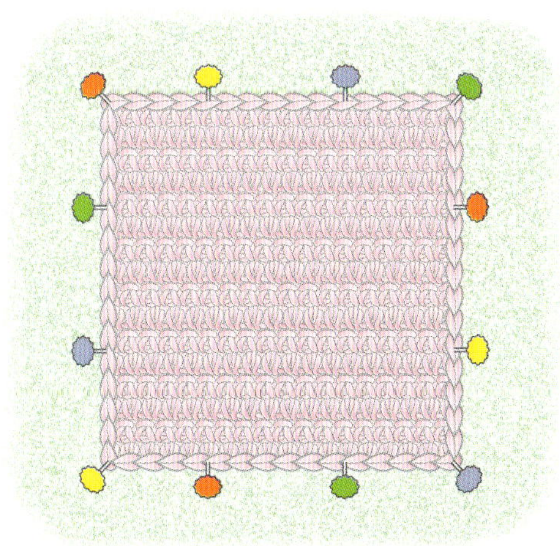

Making an oversewn seam

An oversewn join gives a nice flat seam and is the simplest and most common joining technique.

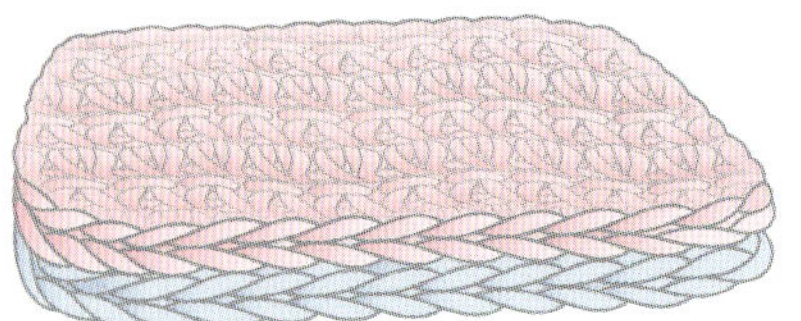

1 Thread a yarn sewing needle with the yarn you're using in the project. Place the pieces to be joined with right sides together.

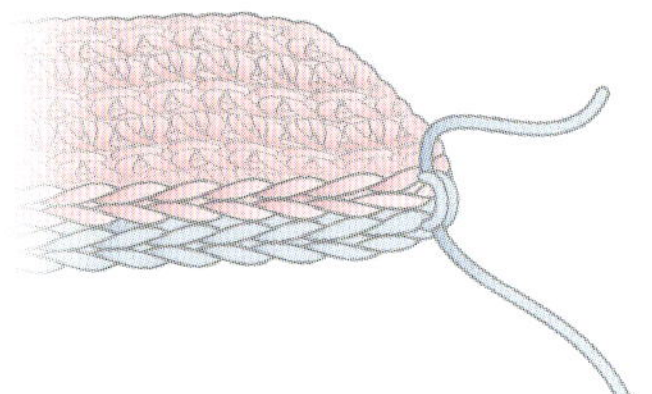

2 Insert the needle in one corner in the top loops of the stitches of both pieces and pull up the yarn, leaving an end of about 2in (5cm). Go into the same place with the needle and pull up the yarn again; repeat two or three times to secure the yarn at the start of the seam.

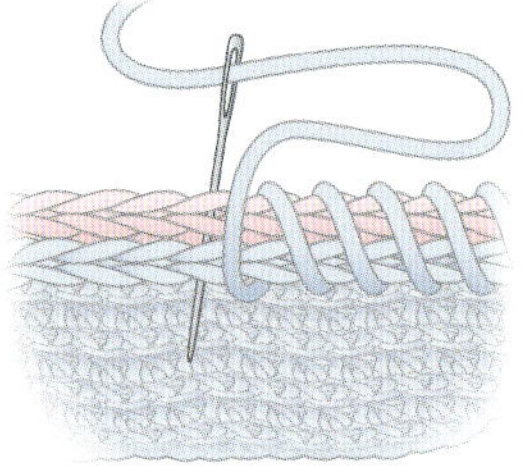

3 Join the pieces together by taking the needle through the loops at the top of the corresponding stitches on each piece to the end. Fasten off the yarn at the end, as in step 2.

Making a single crochet seam

With a single crochet seam you join two pieces together using a crochet hook and working a single crochet stitch through both pieces, instead of sewing them together with a yarn end and a yarn sewing needle. This makes a quick and strong seam and gives a slightly raised finish to the edging. For a less raised seam, follow the same basic technique, but work each stitch in slip stitch rather than single crochet.

1 Start by lining up the two pieces with wrong sides together. Insert the hook in the top 2 loops of the stitch of the first piece, then into the corresponding stitch on the second piece.

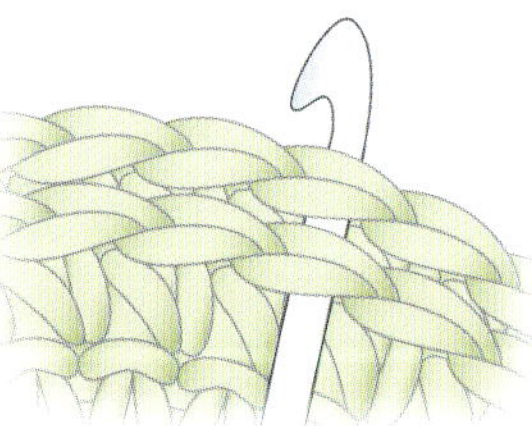

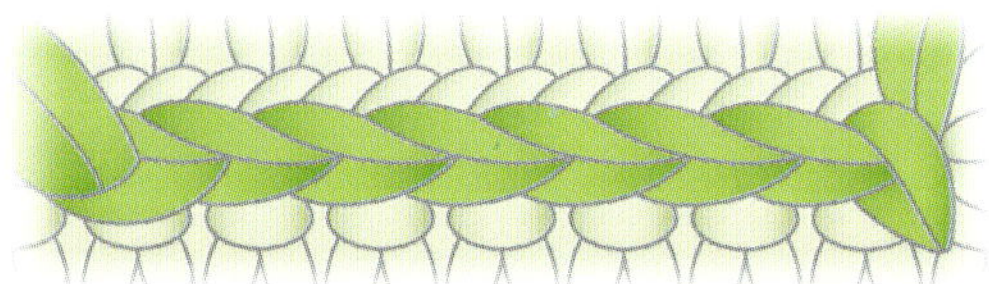

2 Complete the single crochet stitch as normal and continue on the next stitches as directed in the pattern. This gives a raised effect if the single crochet stitches are made on the right side of the work.

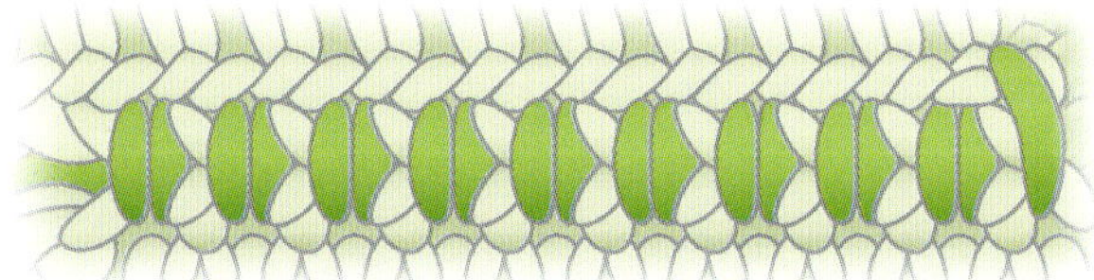

3 You can work with the wrong side of the work facing (with the pieces right side facing) if you don't want this effect and it still creates a good strong join.

Sewing up with whip stitch

Whip stitch is an easy way to join pieces, but you will be able to see the stitches clearly, so use a matching yarn. Lay the two pieces to be joined next to each other with right sides facing upward. Secure the yarn to one piece. Insert the needle into the front of the fabric, then up from the back of the adjoining fabric. Repeat along the seam.

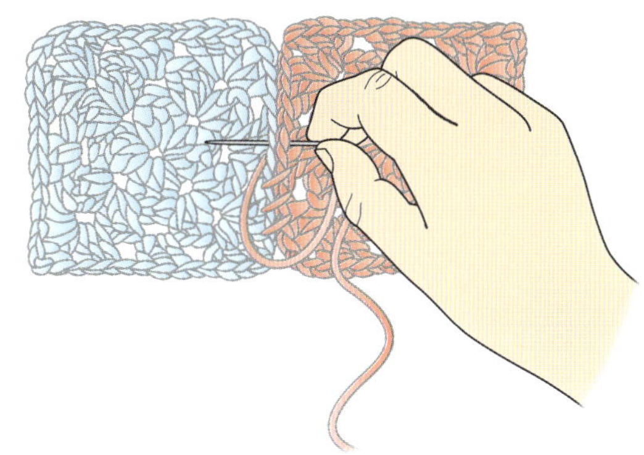

Making pompoms

1 Using a pair of card rings cut to the size of the pompom you would like to create, cut a length of yarn and wind it around the rings until the hole in the center is filled.

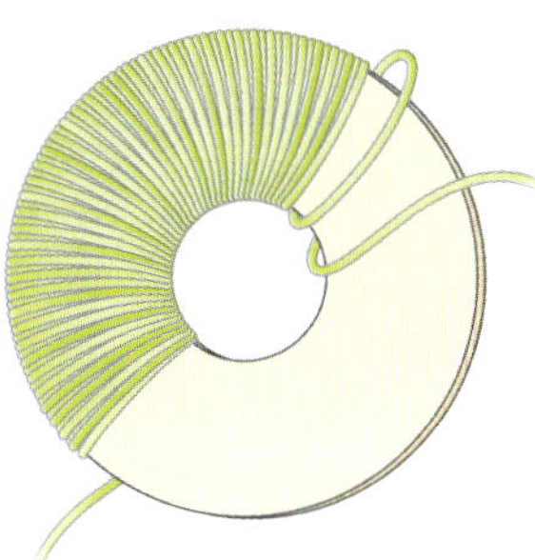

2 Cut through the loops around the outer edge of the rings and ease them slightly apart. Thread a length of yarn between the layers of card and tie tightly, leaving a long end. Remove the card rings and fluff up the pompom. The long yarn end can be used to sew the pompom in place.

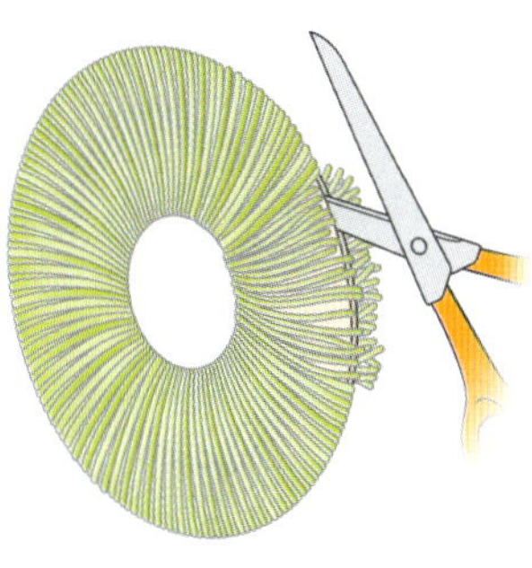

Making tassels

1 Cut yarn to quantity and length given in the pattern. Take suggested bundle of strands and fold in half. With right side of project facing, insert a crochet hook from the wrong side through one of the edge stitches. Catch the bunch of strands with the hook at the fold point.

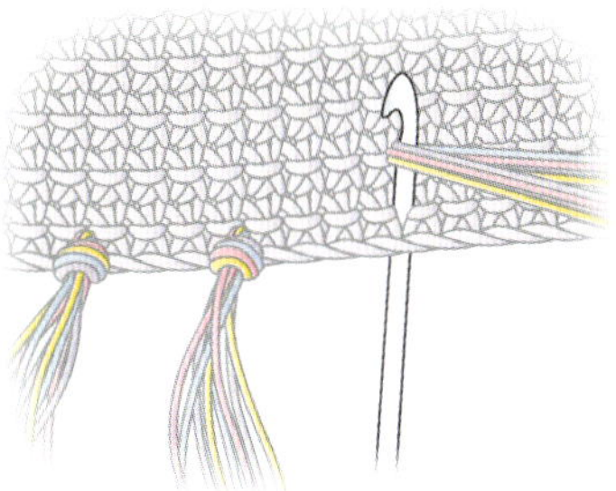

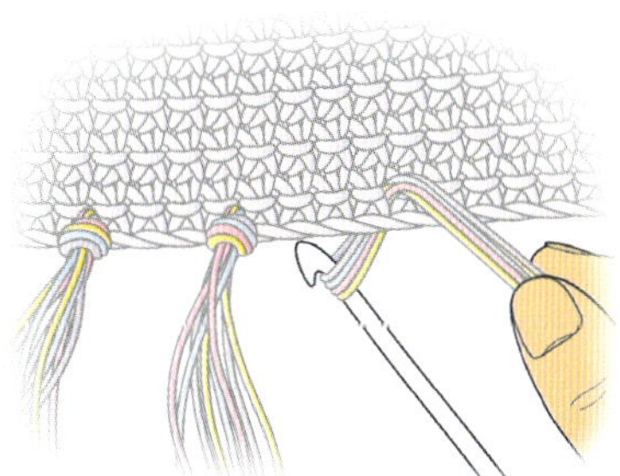

2 Pull the strands on the hook through to make a loop at the back of the work.

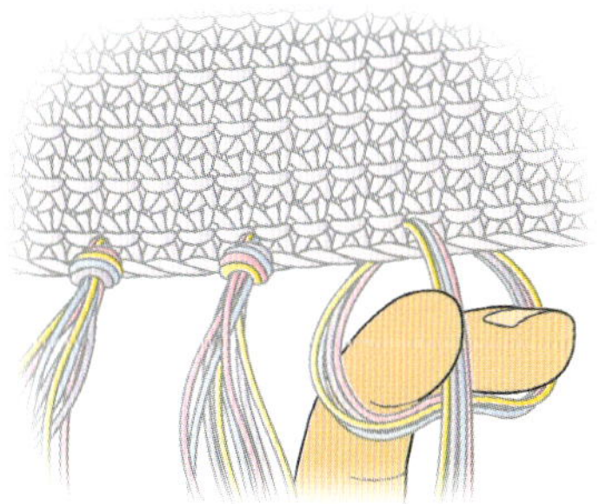

3 With your fingers, make the loop bigger and then pull the ends of the bunch of strands through the loop.

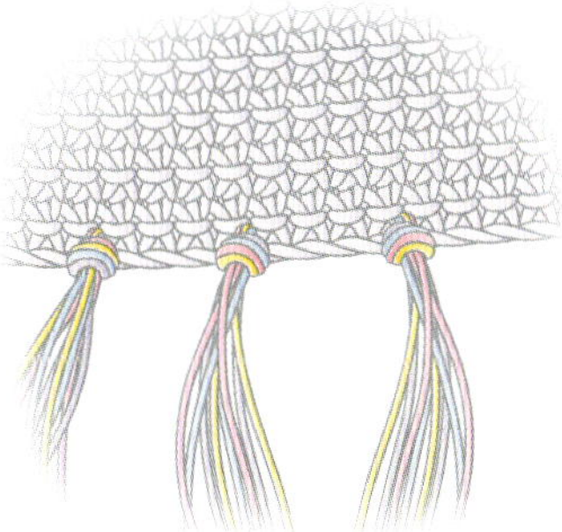

4 Pull on the ends to tighten the loop firmly, and secure the tassel.

Surface crochet

Surface crochet is a simple way to add extra decoration to a finished item, working slip stitches over the surface of the fabric.

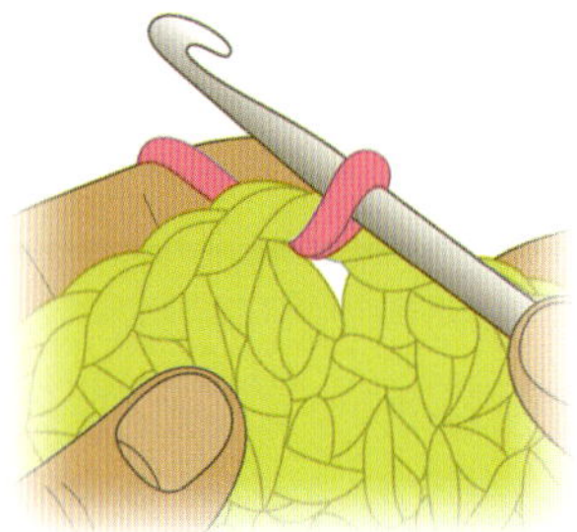

1 Using a contrast yarn, make a slip knot. Holding the yarn with the slip knot behind the work and the hook in front, insert the hook between two stitches from front to the back and catch the slip knot behind the work with the hook. Draw the slip knot back through, so there is 1 loop on the hook at the front of the work.

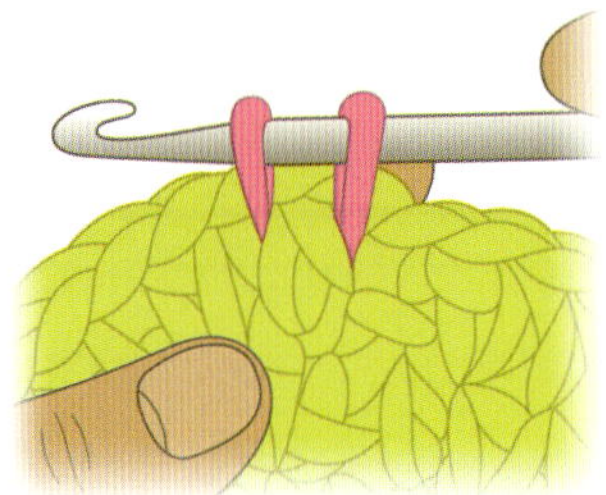

2 Insert the hook between the next 2 stitches, yarn round hook and draw a loop through to the front. You will now have 2 loops on the hook.

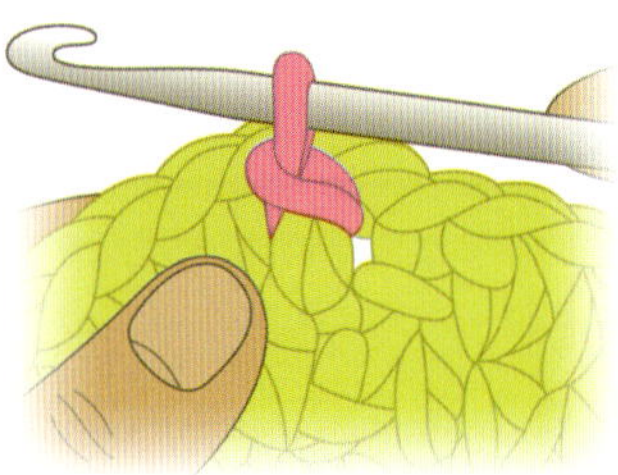

3 Pull the first loop on the hook through the second loop to complete the first slip stitch on the surface of the work.

Repeat steps 2 and 3 to make the next slip stitch. To join two ends with an invisible join, cut the yarn and thread onto a yarn needle. Insert the needle up through the last stitch, into the first stitch as if you were crocheting it, then into the back loop of the previous stitch. Fasten off on the wrong side.

Beading

When using beads, they must all be threaded onto the yarn before you start crocheting. Beads are placed when working with the wrong side of the work facing you. The beads will sit at the back of the work, and so appear on the front (right side).

1 When a bead is needed, slide it up the strand toward the back of the work so it's ready to place in the right part of the stitch you are working.

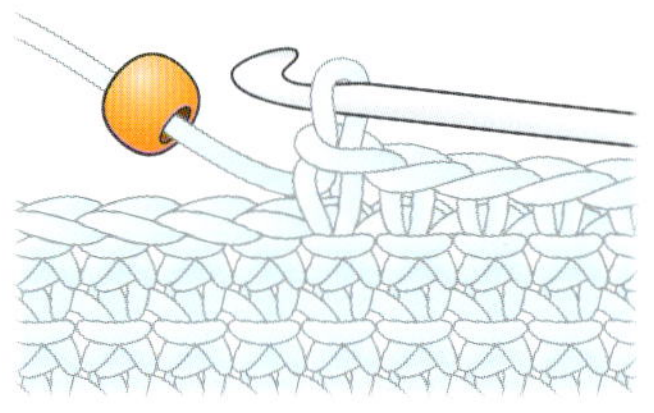

2 Work the stitch as indicated in the pattern. This will secure the bead at the back.

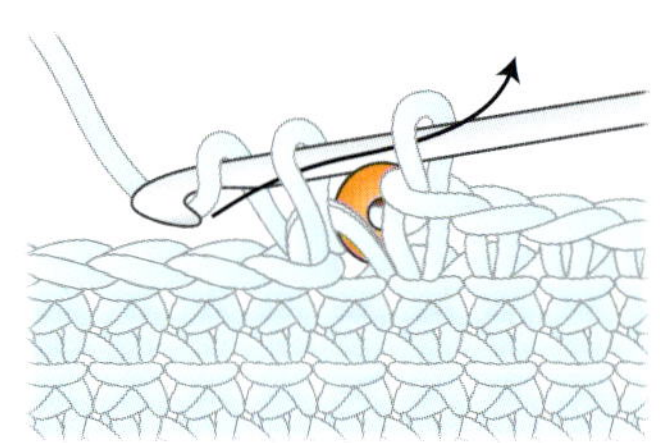

CROCHET STITCH CONVERSION CHART

Crochet stitches are worked in the same way in both the USA and the UK, but the stitch names are not the same and identical names are used for different stitches. Below is a list of the US terms used in this book, and the equivalent UK terms.

US TERM	UK TERM
single crochet (sc)	double crochet (dc)
half double crochet (hdc)	half treble (htr)
double crochet (dc)	treble (tr)
treble (tr)	double treble (dtr)
double treble (dtr)	triple treble (ttr)
triple treble (ttr)	quadruple treble (qtr)
gauge	tension
yarn over hook (yo)	yarn round hook (yrh)

abbreviations

alt alternat(e)ing
approx. approximately
beg begin(ning)
BLO back loop only
BP back post
cm centimeter(s)
cont continu(e)ing
ch chain
dc double crochet
dec decreas(e)ing
dtr double treble
edc elongated double crochet
FLO front loop only
foll follow(s)ing
FP front post
g gram(mes)
hdc half double crochet
in inch(es)
inc increas(e)ing
m meter(s)
mm millimeter(s)
oz ounce(s)
PM place marker
patt pattern
prev previous
rem remaining
rep repeat
RS right side
sc single crochet
sc2tog single crochet 2 stitches together
ss slip stitch
st(s) stitch(es)
sp space
tog together
tr treble
yds yards
WS wrong side
yo yarn over hook
[ ] work section between square brackets number of times stated
***** asterisk indicates beginning of repeated section of pattern

suppliers

The projects in this book are great for using up leftover yarn in your craft supply.

If you wish to accurately substitute a different yarn for the one recommended in the pattern, try the Yarnsub website for suggestions: www.yarnsub.com

I also recommend exploring your local yarn stores to support small business owners and see what treasures you might find.

USA

Knitting Fever Inc.
www.knittingfever.com

WEBS
www.yarn.com

Michaels
Craft supplies
www.michaels.com

AUSTRALIA

Sunspun
Retail store only
(Canterbury, Victoria)
Tel: +61 (0)3 9830 1609

UK

Love Crafts
Yarns and craft supplies
www.lovecrafts.com

Wool
Yarn, hooks
Store in Bath
+44 (0)1225 469144
www.woolbath.co.uk

VV Rouleaux
Ribbons
Store in London
+44 (0)207 627 4455
www.vvrouleaux.com

Laughing Hens
Online sales
Tel: +44 (0) 1829 740903
www.laughinghens.com

John Lewis
Yarns and craft supplies
Telephone numbers of stores on website
www.johnlewis.com

Hobbycraft
Yarns and craft supplies
www.hobbycraft.co.uk

Wool Warehouse
Yarns and craft supplies
www.woolwarehouse.co.uk

YARN COMPANIES

Cascade
Stockist locator on website
www.cascadeyarns.com

DMC
Stockist locator on website
www.dmc.com

Rico Design
Stockist locator on website
www.rico-design.de

Rowan Yarns
Stockist locator on website
www.knitrowan.com

Scheepjes
Stockist locator on website
www.scheepjes.com

Stylecraft
Stockist locator on website
www.stylecraft-yarns.co.uk

acknowledgments

My thanks to Cindy Richards, Penny Craig, Marie Clayton, and the team at CICO books for all your support and to Jemima Bicknell for making me look so professional!

Deepest gratitude to Laura Shipley for igniting the flame. To Michael Armstrong for fanning that flame and being there from the very beginning—your faith and belief in me made all the difference. To my colorful friend Rosie Wilks for her help with the Granny Love Blanket and for making this obsession with yarn seem perfectly normal!

To my "Crazy Correct Ladies" (you know who you are!) who meet every month to hook and drink coffee. To fellow designer Fran Morgan for untangling the knots and Sara Huntington for giving me a chance.

Thank you also to Mirella Lamarina and Christian Henwood for keeping me healthy with their yoga magic and healing touch.

And to my family for putting up with me and my obsession with crochet, especially my nan who planted the seed.

I am profoundly grateful to Rick who competes with my work for space on the sofa, floor, kitchen table, and bed (under and on!). Thank you for your encouragement and tolerance and for pretending to know what I'm talking about when I go full crochet on you!

And lastly to my Instagram friends and fellow crocheters who share their work so generously online… you inspire!

The biggest perk to writing a crochet book (beyond being able to say "I've written a book don't you know!") is being given access to an abundance of yarns. It's been a complete joy and pleasure to have worked so closely with Rico Design and Scheepjes, who have both been so generous—your colors are magical! Thank you also to Stylecraft for supporting this project.

index